SUMMARY

I0429148

Much hyperbole surrounds the political regime in the Democratic People's Republic of Korea (DPRK, or North Korea). Many analysts argue that North Korea is a unique political system. What kind of regime is the DPRK, and what kind of leader does it have?

A variety of labels are given to the North Korean regime. These include likening the regime to an organized crime family and to a corporatist organism. There are certainly merits to each of these approaches, but each has its limitations. Pyongyang does share some of the attributes of organized crime and certainly engages in criminal activity in a systematic and calculating manner. This pattern of illicit behavior includes the production and distribution of narcotics as well as the counterfeiting of foreign currencies, cigarettes, and pharmaceuticals. But the DPRK is more than a crime family — it possesses a massive conventional military force as well as significant strategic forces. Moreover, the regime continues to brainwash, imprison, or starve North Koreans, inflicting untold misery and death on its people. Corporatism, meanwhile, may provide insights into certain aspects of the system, but its utility is limited by the confusion that surrounds understanding of this concept.

Certainly North Korea is distinct politically, but it also has significant commonalities with various regime types and authority structures. Pyongyang is a highly centralized and militarized bureaucratic regime organized around an all-powerful leader. This monograph examines the leader and the system, and identifies the regime type. The author contends that the North Korean political system is best conceived as a totalitarian regime that, although weakened, remains remarkably resilient. After analyzing the key elements of totalitarianism, he argues that the system's greatest test will probably come after the death of Kim Jong Il.

While the totalitarian regime may not long survive Kim's passing, one cannot assume that the system will collapse. Rather, the end of totalitarianism may simply mean that the DPRK will enter a new "post-totalitarian" phase similar to the paths taken by other communist systems such as the Soviet Union and China. While the latter term may be a good fit to describe China's political system in the 1990s and first decade of the 21st century, it seems inaccurate to describe North Korea. North Korea has not undergone any process of "de-Kimification": Kim Il Sung remains a deity in 21st century North Korea and criticism or reappraisal is unthinkable. Moreover, no one has contemplated criticizing or challenging his legacy because, by all accounts, he remains universally revered by DPRK citizens, including defectors. Furthermore, any official reevaluation of Kim Il Sung is extremely unlikely because the regime is currently led by Kim's son. The most accurate way to characterize North Korea today is as an eroding totalitarian regime.

While totalitarianism is a powerful and intimidating system, it places tremendous strain on a state and a society—demanding constant activity and mobilization of personnel and exploitation of resources. The costs of maintaining heightened ideological indoctrination, an ever-vigilant coercive apparatus, and a large national defense organization are high and ultimately debilitating. To maintain this for decades results in fatigue and burnout. Eventually leaders and followers reach a point where both are physically and mentally exhausted, and the country's infrastructure and resources become devastated. North Korea's elite and ordinary people appear to be approaching this point. But this fatigue and burnout does not appear to produce much in the way of protest or dissent, let alone revolt; most likely the majority of people in North Korea are simply too tired to do much more than focus their time and energy on providing for the basic needs of their families.

An absolute dictator still rules the regime. While the regime continues to hold a monopoly of the instruments of coercion, there has been some slippage or erosion in the defining features of totalitarianism. First of all, Kim Jong Il, although he is virtually an absolute dictator, appears to take into account the opinions of others the way his father did not. And ideology no longer appears to be so focused on transforming the state and society and more on the instrumental goals of economic recovery, development, and firming up regime power. While a condition of terror remains palpable, it is no longer all pervasive, and individuals are able to navigate or circumvent the system without fearing that they face dire consequences. As a result of the shift in ideology and alleviation of the climate of terror, the regime has become "corrupted" literally as bribery is rampant, and figuratively as the regime seeks to preserve its power and status. Meanwhile, the Stalinist centrally planned economy has been seriously eroded, and the monopoly of mass communication has loosened significantly. The regime has attempted to repair the latter two elements, but it is not clear to what extent this will be successful.

The regime appears to be stable and not on the brink of collapse. While it is difficult to speculate about the longevity of North Korea as a political entity, it is more manageable to forecast the future of totalitarianism in the DPRK. Totalitarian regimes rarely endure longer than several decades and almost never survive the passing of the absolute dictator. In fact, Pyongyang is unique in that it is the only totalitarian regime to weather a leadership transition (from Kim Il Sung to Kim Jong Il). Indeed, North Korea is the world's "longest lasting totalitarian regime, having spanned some 4 decades and surviving generational leadership succession." Perhaps none of the numerous challenges the regime faces is more daunting than the succession question. Kim has probably at most 10-15 years in which to pave the way for one of his offspring to succeed him. If he lives long enough, it is possible he could be successful. What is less likely is that totalitarianism could survive another leadership transition. At some point, the totalitarian regime will simply collapse or weaken to the extent that it becomes a post-totalitarianism system.

Possibly the clearest indication of the status and fate of Pyongyang's totalitarian regime over the next 10 years or so will come in how the arrangements for the succession to Kim Jong Il are handled. Is there evidence that a particular individual is being groomed to succeed Kim? The answer appears to be "yes." Some other key indicators to monitor are signs of dissent among elites and masses, especially fissures that might occur within the party or military. By carefully charting trends, observers can make it less likely that they will be caught off guard by the actions of North Korea's leader or changes in its political system.

KIM JONG IL AND NORTH KOREA:
THE LEADER AND THE SYSTEM

Much hyperbole surrounds the political regime in the Democratic People's Republic of Korea (DPRK). Much of it focuses on North Korea's enigmatic dictator, Kim Jong Il, and his nuclear program. Certainly, he has been the target of much derision and the butt of many jokes because of his appearance, reclusiveness, and speculation about his predilections. But the Pyongyang regime is more than simply a garden variety dictator who happens to possess weapons of mass destruction (WMD). The DPRK is also a large bureaucratic and organizational entity. This begs the question: What kind of regime is the DPRK, and what kind of leader does it have?

Many analysts argue that North Korea is a unique political system. Certainly, it is distinct politically to the extent that each country has its own specific characteristics. But North Korea also has significant commonalities with various regime types and authority structures. Pyongyang is a highly centralized and militarized bureaucratic regime organized around an all-powerful leader. This monograph examines the leader and the system. The author identifies the regime type and analyzes its key elements. He contends that North Korea's political system is best conceived of as a totalitarian regime that although weakened, remains remarkably resilient. The monograph argues that the greatest test that the system is likely to face will come after the death of Kim Jong Il. While the totalitarian regime may not long survive Kim's passing, one cannot assume that the system will collapse. Rather, the end of totalitarianism may simply mean that the DPRK will enter a new "post-totalitarian" phase similar to the paths taken by other communist systems such as the Soviet Union and China following the passing of Joseph Stalin and Mao Zedong, respectively.

A variety of labels are given to the North Korean regime, including likening it to an organized crime family and to a corporatist organism. North Korea also has been depicted as what might be labeled "fragmented totalitarianism."[1] There are certainly merits to each of these approaches, but each has its limitations. Pyongyang shares some of the attributes of organized crime and certainly engages in criminal activity in a systematic and calculating manner. This pattern of illicit behavior includes the production and distribution of narcotics, notably heroin and methamphetamines, which reportedly provide hundreds of millions of U.S. dollars worth of income to Pyongyang annually. In addition, North Korea is known to engage in the counterfeiting of foreign currencies, cigarettes, and pharmaceuticals.[2] Nevertheless, Pyongyang is much more than a variant of a crime family such as the fictional ones depicted in the Mario Puzo's *The Godfather* or Home Box Office's *The Sopranos*. For a start, neither Don Corleone nor Tony Soprano ran a country about the size of Mississippi, controlled the world's fourth largest military, or could count on the powerful emotional appeal of nationalism to the reinforce the ties of personal and familial loyalty in their organizations (although ethnic loyalty certainly plays a role for both fictional crime bosses).[3] However, as analyst David Asher states: ". . . North Korea has become a 'soprano state' — a government guided by a . . . leadership whose actions, attitudes, and affiliations increasingly resemble those of an organized crime family more than a normal nation." Asher asserts that, as a result: "North Korea is the only government in the world today that can be identified as being actively involved in directing crime as a central part of its national economic strategy and foreign policy."[4]

Moreover, while corporatism may provide insights into certain aspects of the system, its utility is limited by the confusion that surrounds understanding of this concept.[5]

Finally, "fragmented totalitarianism" is a fuzzy term, but "fragmented authoritarianism" does not seem to be much more appropriate. The concept of "fragmented totalitarianism" is problematic since it amounts to an oxymoron: if power is truly fragmented in a regime, then it certainly does not qualify as totalitarian (see Figure 1).[6] A more useful term and concept, post-totalitarianism, is discussed below.

While the latter term may be a good fit to describe China's political system in the 1990s and first decade of the 21st century, it seems inaccurate to describe North Korea that way.[7] For one, North Korea has not undergone any process of "de-Kimification" to parallel the serious reassessment of Mao that China undertook in the late 1970s and early 1980s, let alone the more thorough "De-Stalinization"

TOTALITARIANISM	POST-TOTALITARIANISM
1. Absolute dictator and ruling party (monistic)	Dictator's power weakens (pluralism and dissent emerge)
2. Transformational ideology (totalist/utopian goals)	Instrumental ideology (economic development and party rule)
3. Terror all-pervasive	Terror no longer pervasive
4. Monopoly of coercive apparatus	Monopoly maintained
5. Centrally planned economy	Eroded
6. Monopoly of mass communication	Eroded

no TE: Compiled by author.

Figure 1. Totalitarianism and Post-Totalitarianism.

spearheaded by Soviet leader Nikita Khrushchev in the mid-1950s. Kim Il Sung remains a deity in 21st century North Korea and criticism or reappraisal is unthinkable. Moreover, no one has contemplated criticizing or challenging his legacy because, by all accounts, he remains universally revered by DPRK citizens, including defectors.[8] Furthermore, any official reevaluation of Kim Il Sung is extremely unlikely because the regime is currently led by Kim's son. I contend that the most accurate way to characterize North Korea today is as an eroding totalitarian regime.[9]

TOTALITARIANISM IN ONE FAMILY

The North Korean political system most closely approximates totalitarianism.[10] It possesses the six characteristics of totalitarianism identified by Carl Friedrich and Zbigniew Brzezinski half a century ago. The DPRK has an absolute dictator and mass party, an elaborate ideology, its people live in a condition of terror under the thumb of an extremely repressive coercive apparatus with a centralized economy, and the regime exerts almost total control over the mediums of mass communication.[11]

A central element of the regime and the critical element of the coercive apparatus is the military. North Korea's military is not examined in this monograph but will be the focus of the next monograph in this series. Suffice it here to make two observations. First, the DPRK is "undoubtedly the most militarized . . . [regime] on earth."[12] Second, although communist regimes are typically dubbed "party-states" (because the communist party and government bureaucracies tend to be heavily intertwined or enmeshed), it is more accurate to call these regimes "party-military-states" to underscore the prominent role routinely played by the armed forces.[13] In short, the role of the military in North Korea is so important that it merits a monograph devoted exclusively to the subject. The political landscape of the DPRK is dominated by three massive bureaucratic organizations (see Figure 2): "the Party" (the Korean Workers' Party, or KWP), "the State" (the DPRK), and "the Military" (the Korean People's Army, KPA, or Army).

Although the extreme degree of control and repression that existed while Kim Il Sung was alive has weakened noticeably, today North Korea remains a country where the regime seeks to control not only what the populace does, but also what it thinks. However, the DPRK has not evolved into post-totalitarianism yet. Post-totalitarianism is markedly weaker than totalitarianism but still distinct from and more powerful than authoritarianism (Figure 1).

Under post-totalitarianism, regime control loosens significantly and the dictator's power weakens, ideology ceases to be "transformational" and terror is no longer all-pervasive, while central planning and the monopoly of mass communication both erode. But the coercive apparatus remains firmly in place.[14] By this yardstick, North Korea is not there just yet: Kim Jong Il may feel that his power is not as absolute as his father's and ideology may be shifting from transformational to instrumental, but the DPRK has not entered post-totalitarianism. The regime leadership has yet to shift its ideological emphasis from "utopia" to "development."[15] Pluralism and dissent have not yet emerged (although these manifestations may not be so far off) and the coercive apparatus still seems largely effective (with some exceptions), but a condition of terror appears to be rather less pervasive. One clear manifestation of these changes is that Pyongyang is no longer capable of preventing migration within the country or out migration to China by hungry or starving people. It is estimated that hundreds of

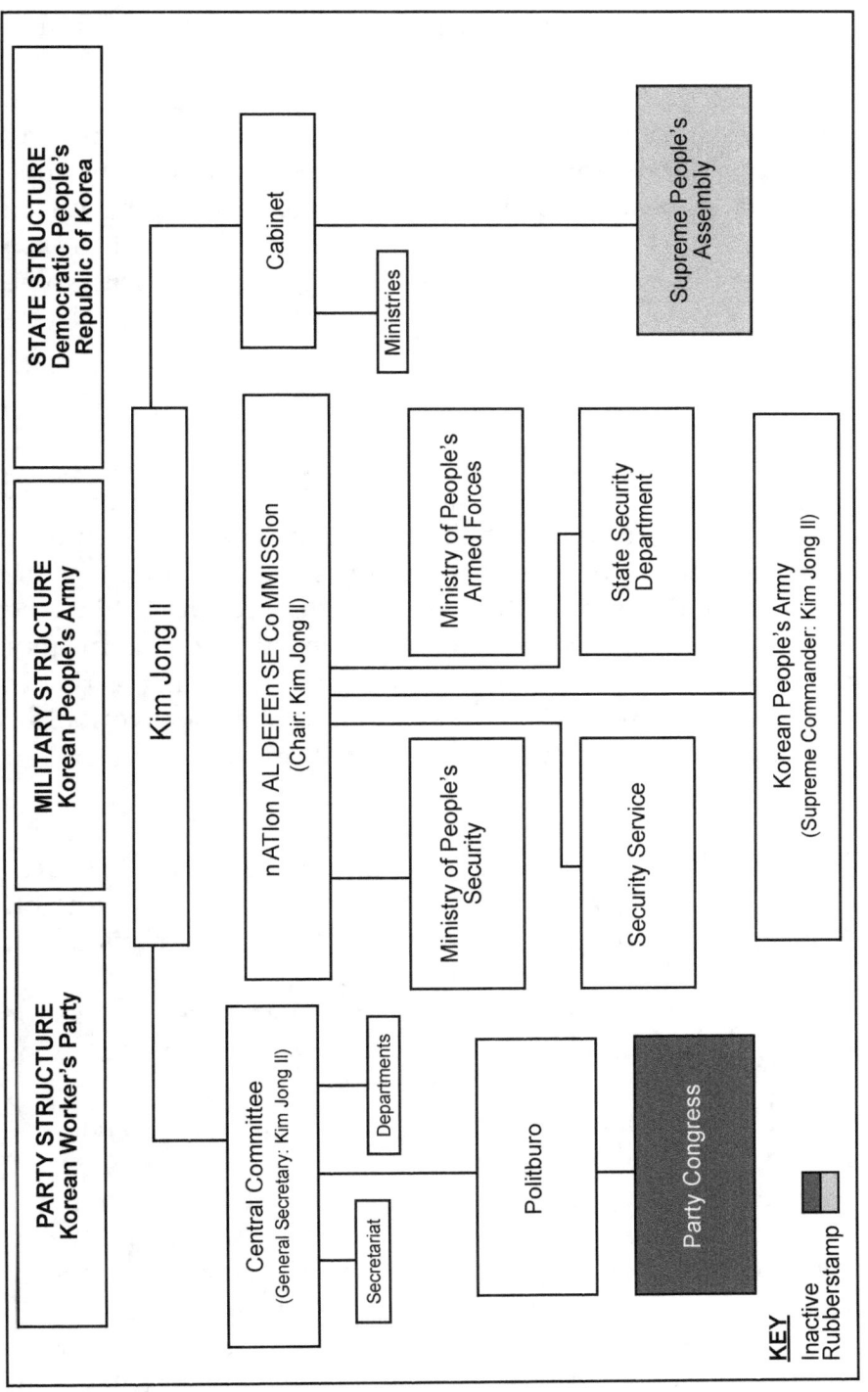

PARTY STRUCTURE
Korean Worker's Party

MILITARY STRUCTURE
Korean People's Army

STATE STRUCTURE
Democratic People's Republic of Korea

Kim Jong Il

Cabinet

Ministries

Supreme People's Assembly

nATIon AL DEFEn SE Co MMISSIon
(Chair: Kim Jong Il)

Ministry of People's Armed Forces

State Security Department

Ministry of People's Security

Security Service

Korean People's Army
(Supreme Commander: Kim Jong Il)

Central Committee
(General Secretary: Kim Jong Il)

Departments

Secretariat

Politburo

Party Congress

KEY
Inactive
Rubberstamp

no TE: Compiled by author from numerous sources.

Figure 2: The Party-Military-State.

thousands of North Koreans have traversed the country in search of food and 100,000 or more people have sought at least temporary refuge in China. Moreover, thousands have attempted to defect, mostly via China.[16] While North Korea's centrally planned economy has eroded considerably over the past decade or so, it remains alive and the regime appears to be in the process of reactivating it (see below). The DPRK's monopoly of mass communication has also been under assault, but the regime has been fighting back with some success.

Absolute Dictator and Mass Party.

Kim Jong Il appears very much in control of North Korea. While there have been periodic reports since Kim Il Sung's death in July 1994 that the younger Kim's power and influence were eroding, there is no firm indication that this was or is the case. In late 2004, for example, speculation was rampant about the reason behind the removal of many public portraits of Kim Jong Il. Did this mean a scaling back of the cult of personality or possibly that a power struggle was underway?[17] Many reporters and analysts overlooked a more mundane explanation: that the portraits may have been taken down for cleaning or updating.[18]

According to those who have first-hand experience dealing with Kim Jong Il, he seems to be in firm control of North Korea. Madeleine Albright reported that Kim answered 14 questions on North Korea's missile program posed by the Clinton administration in her presence by himself without once "consulting the expert by his side."[19] Moreover, Hwang Jong Yop, the highest level defector from Pyongyang who had many years to observe Kim's behavior and grasp the structure of power in North Korea, stated: "Who is in charge? No one [else] has real power. . . . Only Kim Jong Il has real power. . . ."[20]

Kim Jong Il did engage in a decades-long effort to claim his father's mantle, and the dynastic transition from Kim the father to Kim the son seems to have been quite smooth.[21] This is not altogether surprising, given that the elder Kim began making preparations for the hereditary succession as early as 1972 and the younger Kim spent at least 22 years as an "understudy."[22] The younger Kim's rare appearances and apparent reluctance to speak in public perhaps reflect a combination of the so-called "successor's dilemma" and a desire to project appropriate Confucian deference for a father by his son rather than shyness or a dislike of being on display.[23] The dilemma means that while the heir apparent tries to prepare for the day when he/she will assume the top position of leadership, he/she is careful not to overshadow or antagonize the older leader and remain sufficiently deferential. This dynamic has proved challenging for leadership successions in other communist systems such as China.[24] In the case of North Korea, successor Kim seemed very adept at handling this dilemma. According to Dae Sook Suh: "Kim Jong Il was careful not to upstage his father."[25] The younger Kim skillfully followed his "survival strategy."[26]

Kim Jong Il: The Hardest Working Man in Show Business. Perceptions of Kim Jong Il have undergone a metamorphosis from the image of a reclusive playboy to that of a driven dictator. Rumors abounded about his drinking, womanizing, and penchant for fast cars. But in recent years, Kim has undergone a dramatic public relations makeover, becoming a personable and engaging tyrant: a thinking man, well-informed, with a hands-on leadership style.[27]

He proved a gracious host to Republic of Korea President Kim Dae Jung in mid-2000 and several months later to then Secretary of State Madeleine Albright when each visited Pyongyang. Visitors invariably remark on the charm and conversation skills of their North Korean host. Albright reports that her meetings with Kim in late-2000 confirmed reports from Chinese, Russian, and South Korean sources that he was "knowledgeable, good humored, and relatively normal." The former Secretary of State, who had the opportunity to engage in extended discussions with the dictator and observe her host's behavior during a 2-day visit to Pyongyang, remarked that, while Kim was "isolated, [he was] not uninformed," and impressed her as "an intelligent man who knew what he wanted."[28]

So *what* does Kim Jong Il *want*?[29] Kim appears to have big plans for his country: he apparently has a vision of North Korea becoming a high technology Mecca: he visited China's Silicon Valley on the outskirts of Beijing in 2001. His most senior military leader, Marshal Jo Myon Rok, visited the original Silicon Valley in 2000 during a brief California stopover on the return leg of his trip to meet President Bill

Clinton in the White House. Kim reportedly keeps well-informed by watching Cable News Network and surfing the worldwide web. For some reason, he asked Madeleine Albright for the address of the Department of State's website.[30]

The key events in his metamorphosis from reclusive playboy to driven dictator occurred in 2000: the summit he held with President Kim Dae Jung of the Republic of Korea in Pyongyang in mid-June and the late October visit to North Korea of Secretary of State Albright. The most impressive performance was his gracious hosting of the inter-Korea summit in June 2000: what I call "Kim Jong Il's coming out party." President Kim traveled to Pyongyang for an historic meeting between the leaders of two Koreas. The North Korean leader displayed a confident, rational, and amicable public persona that shattered the prevailing image of him as a reclusive and manic eccentric.[31] This impressive public relations effort to promote a certain image to the North Korea people, to South Korea (Kim was appropriately deferential to his older guest from Seoul), and the world probably makes Kim worthy of the label "the hardest working man in show business."

In a very real sense, Kim Jong Il is engaged in the essence of show business: writing scripts, directing casts, building sets, and playing the leading roles himself in major cinematic and theatrical productions. All of this is done in order to project an image and a storyline—a version of "reality"—that is believable, credible, and appealing to his foreign and/or domestic audiences. Kim appears to be the producer, director, and leading man in his own feature film.[32] The epic is without parallel in terms of the scope, expense, and sustained effort that goes into production. By most accounts, Kim has a long held fascination with movie making. His first post of any real responsibility under his father was in charge of propaganda (See Figure 3). In this position he oversaw the production of movies.[33] His determination to produce quality full length feature films drove him to arrange the kidnapping of renowned South Korean movie director Shin Sang Ok and his actress ex-wife Choi Eun Hee in 1978. He reportedly has a huge film collection and by his own admission regularly watches foreign movies.[34] Kim also takes an interest in entertainment/propaganda extravaganzas. He told Albright that he choreographed the Las Vegas-style showgirl stage show provided as after dinner entertainment for the visiting chief U.S. diplomat.[35] Kim probably also had a major hand in designing the massive Nuremburg-style rally at the stadium that Albright witnessed the day before.

1941: Kim Jong Il born in Soviet Far East and lives there in early years of life
1949: Mother dies
1950-52: Lives in China during Korean War
1959: Visits Moscow with his father
1964: Graduates from Kim Il Sung University and becomes #2 official in Korean
     Workers' Party (KWP) Propaganda Department
1972: Designated as successor by father
1973: Appointed to direct KWP's Organization Department
1980: Appointed to KWP's Politburo and to 2nd ranking position on KWP's
     Military Commission
1983: Visits China
1992: Promoted to Marshal and supreme commander of Korean People's Army
1993: Appointed chair of National Defense Council
1994: Kim Il Sung dies
1997: Becomes Chair of the KWP
2000: Visits China (May), holds summit with South Korean President Kim Dae
     Jung (June), hosts visits by Russian President Putin (July) and U.S.
     Secretary of State Albright (o ctober)
2001: Visits China (January) and Russia (July-August) and hosts visit by Chinese
     leader Jiang Zemin (September)
2002: Visits Russia (August), and hosts visit by Japanese Prime Minister Koizumi
     (September)
2004: Visits China (April), and hosts visit by Japanese Prime Minister Koizumi (May)
2005: Hosts President Hu Jintao of China (o ctober)
2006: Visits China (January)

no TE: Compiled by author from numerous sources.

Figure 3. A Kim Jong Il Timeline.

Kim also appears to be very engaged in ruling North Korea— constantly issuing directives and making telephone calls.[36] He probably adopted these micromanagement tendencies from his father.[37] One recent assessment of Kim Jong Il described him as "Jimmy Carter on an authoritarian tear."[38] This parallel with Jimmy Carter may actually be both an accurate and appropriate one, although not in the flippant way that the author had intended: the characterization appears intended to reassure readers. Whereas on the face of it, this appears to put Kim in a somewhat positive light, delving more into the implications of this depiction puts a more disconcerting and even alarming spin on it.

Former president Jimmy Carter is without a doubt an extremely bright man, a dedicated public servant, and an outstanding humanitarian. Arguably, however, these fine attributes did not make him the most effective president.[39] Carter had a reputation, perhaps undeserved, as a micro manager who, unwilling to delegate, immersed himself in mastering the details and minutiae of an issue.[40] Moreover, according to some accounts, Carter was also, belying his "aw shucks" easy-going common man persona, "[a] man of abundant self-confidence in his own abilities. . . ." At the very least, according to one presidential scholar: "Carter [had] acquired or let show a high degree of arrogance [as president-elect] . . . and during the early months of his presidency."[41]

If the parallel between Carter and Kim in this regard is even partially appropriate or accurate, this is a frightening and even terrifying thought: a Carteresque leader in Pyongyang, but without any of the Georgian's moral scruples, who operates in a system devoid of any democratic checks and balances. Surrounded and advised by sycophants, it is highly unlikely that Kim gets the kind of truthful reporting he desperately needs to make the best decisions. The North Korean leader is probably aware of this problem and tries to compensate by adopting a variety of means. These include his own informal network of informers around the country who report "directly to his office,"[42] and his well-known habit of visiting locales for impromptu "on-the-spot-guidance" appearances. While these efforts may help mitigate the problem, they have their limits and could even exacerbate it in some ways.

In his appearances around the country, it may not be so easy for Kim Jong Il to counter the "Potemkin Village effect." A Potemkin Village is a false construct intended to fool a visiting leader or dignitary by portraying a picturesque or idyllic setting of a village, farm, factory, or military unit to mask a far less pleasant reality.[43] There is a long history in communist regimes and dictatorships generally of parading dignitaries through specially constructed showpieces. Even savvy dictators, including Mao Zedong, have been fooled by these efforts, so it is very likely that Kim Jong Il and his father have been fooled also.[44] The North Korean capital city of Pyongyang might be best categorized as a "Potemkin City" where nothing is as it seems.[45] Journalist and author Bradley Martin writes that he strongly suspected that the full-time jobs of some North Korean citizens are riding the subways all day. The purpose of this is to give the impression of a modern, efficient, and dynamic city.[46] The same may be true of a showpiece hospital on the itinerary for foreign visitors to Pyongyang.[47] It is not clear if Kim Jong Il succumbs to the deceptions of his own regime.

A Rational Leader. However quirky Kim Jong Il is, he is not crazy. He is quite rational, although his calculus of rationality is probably "bounded" by the specific context of his North Korea environment and his (mis)perceptions of the conditions inside and outside his country.[48] In other words, Kim seems to make decisions based on his own evaluation of reality, although his assessment of reality and decisionmaking calculus are distinct and limited by his own experience and exposure to the outside world. The preceding paragraph has discussed the North Korean dictator's state of knowledge about the situation inside his own country. What about his level of knowledge and understanding about the world beyond its borders?

While Kim has made visits overseas, with the exception of childhood sojourns in the Soviet Far East (where he was born) and China (for about 2 years during the Korea War), these have been few, brief, and limited to a handful of countries. In 1957 Kim visited Moscow with his father, and 2 years later he accompanied his father to Eastern European capitals. The Younger Kim has made at least two further visits to Russia (in 2001 and 2002), and at least five visits to China (in 1983, 2000, 2001, 2004, and 2006).[49] During visits to Russia and China, most of the time Kim remained inside a cocoon—a train specially fitted with all the comforts and security of home.[50] Kim has hinted that he has made secret trips to other countries, including Indonesia.[51] Other than through actual visits, his information and impressions of other countries and cultures are likely gleaned from movies, the internet, and satellite television.[52] But even granting that Kim has done more traveling overseas than we are aware of, the question remains why he has not done so more often and publicly. He may not enjoy traveling, especially air travel (he has a strong preference for train travel), he may not like to be out of the country for too long (either because of his need to micromanage, or out of concern that a power vacuum might develop or be filled in his absence). Another reason might be that he feels uncomfortable venturing outside of the world's largest film set where stage effects are out of his control.

Why has he yet to visit Seoul more than 5 years after he accepted Republic of Korea (ROK) President Kim Dae Jung's invitation to go south "at an appropriate time in the future"? Why has he not visited the United States or even expressed an interest in going? The answer to these questions might be that he fears for his safety.[53] Kim is very likely concerned about the threat of assassination. This may explain why he insists on secrecy regarding his trips both at home and abroad. Another answer might be that he believes he has nothing to gain from such trips. Kim Dae Jung has noted that the most controversial part of the joint statement issued at the conclusion of the inter-Korean summit of June 2000 was the sentence mentioning that Kim Jong Il expressed a willingness to visit Seoul. The North Korean leader reportedly told his South Korean counterpart that there were people in North Korea who would strongly oppose such a trip.[54] Another reason for his reluctance to visit Seoul or Washington might be that, in East Asian cultures, it is usually subordinate leaders that travel to visit their superiors and not the other way around.[55] Thus, visitors to Pyongyang appear to be supplicants to the Dear Leader whereas when Kim visits other capitals, he can be can be cast in the role of supplicant. This may help explain why Kim insists on considerable secrecy and a media blackout of his activities when he travels abroad.

In my view, the only way one can conclude Kim Jong Il is "crazy" or a "madman" is if we fall into the trap of mirror imaging and assume that a political leader in Pyongyang thinks like a political leader in Washington or London. While Kim may not necessarily appear to be always acting rationally on the world stage, he is acting rationally within the context of the North Korean political system and his own frame of reference. Of course, all national leaders operate in at least two arenas; that of domestic politics and that of international politics. Kim is no exception in playing two-level games.

But this begs the question: If the North Korean leader was indeed crazy, how would one know it? If one makes the presumption that

Kim Jong Il is the key decisionmaker in Pyongyang, then one assumes that the decisions the regime executes are his. If we consider regime decisions since at least the death of Kim Il Sung in mid-1994, the record is quite impressive. Kim Jong Il has managed to complete a successful leadership succession and stay in power for more than a decade; he has maintained his regime, and in the process ridden out a severe famine and managed (but certainly far from resolved) a systemic economic crisis; and he has adeptly juggled his country's relations with neighboring countries and great powers, most notably the United States, while extracting cash and various forms of aid, including food and fuel, without having to make much in the way of concrete concessions in return. In short, dealt an extremely weak hand of cards, Kim has proved to be an extremely skillful poker player.

Finally, before putting the issue of Kim's rationality to rest, it may be instructive to compare Kim to other absolute dictators from the tyrant hall of infamy who ruled totalitarian regimes. If Kim is crazy, he is crazy the way Joseph Stalin and Mao Zedong were crazy — "like a fox"![56] The North Korean leader is skilled at manipulating and controlling people. It would be a mistake to dismiss Kim's drinking parties as simply evidence of his debauchery and excesses. Rather, as former Pyongyang insider Hwang Jong Yop incisively observes, these occasions should be seen as "an important element of Kim Jong Il's style of politics." These events provide important opportunities for him to reaffirm his status and authority over key subordinates and promote a sense of loyalty and camaraderie among his core supporters.[57] These functions provide a way for attendees to verify that they are regime insiders — in essence the Dear Leader's anointed few. These drinking parties are similar to the types of male bonding activities hosted by government and business leaders in other East Asian countries, including Japan and South Korea, to cement and maintain relationships in the workplace.[58]

Kim also deliberately tries to keep people off balance and guessing about his next move. These efforts are all aimed at making him appear formidable and even dangerous. Kim reportedly remarked: "We must create an environment as if surrounded by fog so our enemies cannot see us directly and clearly."[59] Kim Jong Il, like the deceased leaders of the former Soviet Union and China, appears to be a master of political survival: despite famines and various crises — foreign and domestic — he remains in power. And like Stalin and Mao, he has been quite successful at developing a nuclear weapons program (building, of course, upon his father's efforts).[60] But Kim does not appear to be crazy in the self-destructive way that, say Hitler, proved to be. The Nazi leader proved far less adept at knowing his limitations and limitations of German national power than the infamous above-mentioned communist Soviet and Chinese dictators, both of whom died in their beds of natural causes with their regimes intact. Kim might well possess most, if not all, of the core characteristics of "malignant narcissism." However, this does not necessarily mean that such a personality disorder will prove fatal.[61]

Kim appears eccentric, egotistical, ruthless, and extremely ambitious.[62] His peculiar tastes in Western fashion and fascination with show business and the arts make for an odd mix. Observers often comment on his penchant for platform shoes and bouffant hair styles, almost certainly intended to make him appear taller that his five foot-two inch stature.[63]

Kim is also egotistical, appearing to subscribe to Louis XIV's dictum: "I am the state" [L' etat c'est moi.]. In short, he believes that he personifies North Korea and, by extension, the hopes and aspirations of the entire Korean people. And following this, he believes that he should be succeeded by one of his own offspring. Kim is also, in the words of Bradley Martin, an "insensitive and brutal despot."[64] He has ruthlessly purged those whom he deems to be disloyal or competitors, retains a vast gulag system, and seems unmoved by the mass starvation and continued malnourishment of his people. Finally, he appears to be extremely ambitious and relatively unfazed by the significant setbacks his regime has experienced over the past 15 years. He continues to believe that his regime can survive and recover from its ordeals. He seems to believe that North Korea should continue to have a "civilian" nuclear program at least as much out a matter of national pride and prestige as for purposes of energy security. In Kim's mind, all advanced countries — including Japan and South Korea — have nuclear power, at least for peaceful purposes. Since the DPRK is an advanced country and a major power, it stands to reason that North Korea must possess a nuclear power industry.

There is perhaps no better gauge of Kim's confidence in the continuation of the regime than indications of plans and preparations for a dynastic succession. Kim has at least three sons and two daughters (born to three different mothers) to select from to succeed him as the leader of the regime: an eldest son born in 1971, two other sons born in 1981 and 1983, and two daughters, one born in 1974 and another born in 1987 (see Figure 4). While it does appear that Kim is preparing the way for one of his offspring to succeed him, it is not yet clear which one has been anointed. Speculation about the most likely candidate abounds, especially after an October 2, 2002, essay appeared in the *Nodong Shinmun*, the official newspaper of the KWP, seemed intended to pave the way. The essay claimed: "Already a long time ago, the late Kim Il Sung expressed his determination to win the final victory of the Korean revolution by his son, if not by himself, or by his grandson, if not by his son. President Kim Il Sung reportedly expressed this determination at the secret camp on Mount Paektu in the spring of 1943."[65]

As paramount leader, Kim Jong Il is virtually an absolute dictator, but he does not appear to be worshiped like his father was. Defectors invariably say while they admired and revered Kim Il Sung, they are indifferent or even contemptuous of Kim Jong Il.[66] Thus the charismatic legitimacy of the younger Kim seems to be minimal, if not nonexistent. But for the time being, this seems to be more than offset by the traditional and, perhaps, to a lesser extent the rational-legal basis of his authority to rule North Korea (the traditional dimensions of Kim's legitimacy are discussed in more detail below in the section on ideology).

This discussion raises questions about the likelihood of Kim Jong Il being able to engineer successfully a hereditary succession. Leadership succession has been an insurmountable obstacle for totalitarian regimes and an enormous challenge for communist political systems. North Korea is remarkable as the sole exception: the only totalitarian regime to survive a succession.[67] Therefore, while the chances of a successful dynastic succession occurring in the 21st century North Korea may be daunting, the possibility should not be dismissed out of hand.[68] Indeed, in late 2005 there was considerable speculation that Kim Jong Il is grooming his second eldest son, Kim Jong Chol, as his successor (Figure 4). Recent indications of this

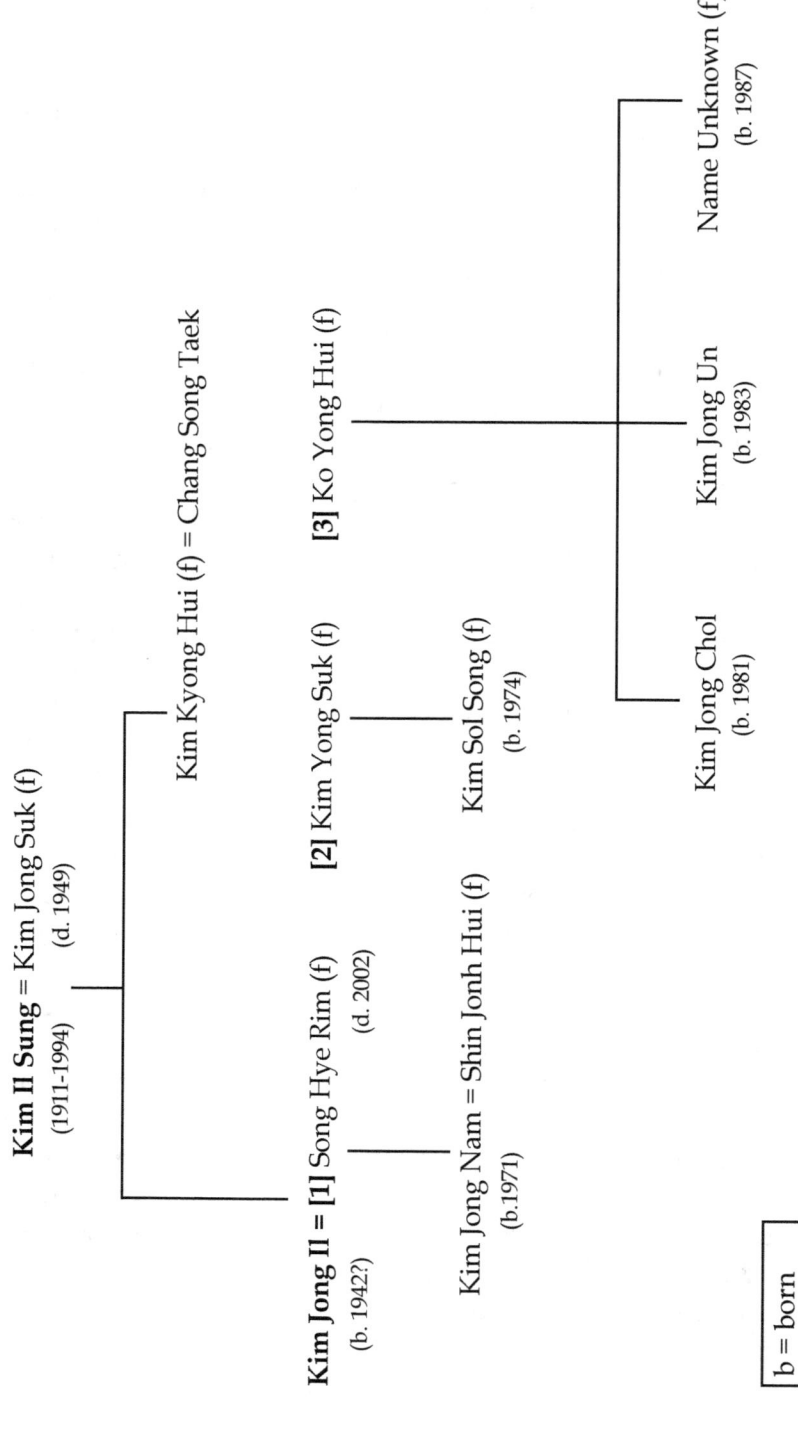

Kim Il Sung = Kim Jong Suk (f)
(1911-1994)   (d. 1949)

Kim Kyong Hui (f) = Chang Song Taek

Kim Jong Il = [1] Song Hye Rim (f)
(b. 1942?)   (d. 2002)

[2] Kim Yong Suk (f)

[3] Ko Yong Hui (f)

Kim Jong Nam = Shin Jonh Hui (f)
(b.1971)

Kim Sol Song (f)
(b. 1974)

Kim Jong Chol
(b. 1981)

Kim Jong Un
(b. 1983)

Name Unknown (f)
(b. 1987)

Figure 4. The Kim Family.

b = born
d = died
(f) = female

no TE: Compiled by author.

16

- Song Hye Rim: mother of Kim Jong Il's eldest son, Jong nam. A north Korean actress and estranged from Kim Jong Il. Lived in Moscow until her death in 2002.
- Kim Yong Suk: mother of Kim Jong Il's favorite daughter, Sol Song.
- Ko Yong Hui: mother of three of Kim Jong Il's three children: Jong Chol, Jong Un and a daughter.
- Kim Jong nam: eldest son of Kim Jong Il. Jong nam studied in Moscow and Geneva. He reportedly speaks French, English, and Russian. Believed to travel abroad frequently under assumed names, he was deported from Japan in 2001 when he was discovered to be traveling on a forged Dominican Republic passport. He is believed to be married with a young son. A possible candidate to succeed his father.
- Kim Jong Chol: second oldest son of Kim Jong Il. Jong Chol reportedly studied in Europe and is believed to be working in the Propaganda Department of the Korean Workers' Party. A possible candidate to succeed his father.
- Kim Jong Un: youngest son of Kim Jong Il. Little is known about him.
- name Unknown: daughter of Kim Jong Il, and sister of Jong Chol and Jong Un.
- Kim Sol Song: favorite daughter of Kim Jong Il. Sol Song followed in her father's footsteps, studied political economy at Kim Il Sung University. She has accompanied her father on inspection tours in North Korea.

Source: Martin, *Under the Loving Care of the Fatherly Leader*, chapter 37.

Figure 4. The Kim Family (concluded).

include the purported creation in 2004, of two new offices in the KWP to promote and prepare the 20-something youngster for his future role and rumors that Jong Chol was introduced to visiting Chinese President Hu Jintao during the latter's visit to Pyongyang in October 2005.[69]

The Korean Workers' Party. Officially founded on October 10, 1945, the KWP is formally the ruling party of the DPRK. Perhaps a more significant date might be August 29, 1946, when the Korean Communist Party-North Korean Bureau, led by Kim Il Sung and the New People's Party under Kim Tu Bong merged to form the KWP. According to historian Charles Armstrong, the new entity, numbering several hundred thousand members, "immediately embarked on an energetic program of recruitment and organizational growth."[70] The

KWP began as a classic Leninist party that adheres to the cardinal principle of democratic centralism. In theory, this principle means that debate and discussion are permitted, but once the top leadership makes a decision, then everyone must observe iron discipline and follow the party line. This principle is intended to ensure strong party unity. The KWP itself is supposed to be governed by a Political Bureau (or Politburo) that is formally elected by a Central Committee which, in turn, has been formally elected by a Party Congress. Delegates to a congress are supposed to have been elected by party cells.

The reality is somewhat different, as the top party leaders tend to rule in an extremely authoritarian style. Senior leaders select supporters to fill positions in these lower organs, and these supporters, in turn, vote for the leaders who selected them. Hence this power structure is dubbed the "circular flow of power."[71] And in the early decades of communist rule, a single leader tends to assume total control of the entire party, and therefore the state and society, and brook no dissent or opposition either inside or outside the party. Communist leaders have taken seriously the belief that the ruling party serves as a "dictatorship of the proletariat" as they go about the serious business of "building socialism." What this has meant in practice is the construction of a powerful and centralized party-state, focusing in particular on a crash program of heavy industrialization and equipping a sizeable and heavily armed military as rapidly as possible. This political structure became known as a Leninist party system after the first leader to construct and control the Bolshevik prototype establishment in the Soviet Union — Vladimir I. Lenin.

In the case of North Korea, the KWP regime was initially installed in 1945 and controlled by the Soviets for some 5 years.[72] While Soviet occupation forces withdrew in 1947-48, in mid-June 1950, on the eve of the Korean War, there were reportedly "as many as 4,000 advisors" in Pyongyang.[73] The leader that gradually emerged as the most important figure (and the one that the Soviets accepted) was Kim Il Sung.[74] Kim soon proved himself to be a quick study. Not only was he eager to amass the total power of the party in his own hands, but he was keen to establish the credentials of the DPRK as an indigenous Korean communist regime independent of foreign control or domination. After a period of Soviet tutelage, Kim launched himself and his regime onto a more autonomous trajectory, seeking to free the KWP from Soviet and Chinese domination. But this did not mean he shunned Soviet and Chinese assistance. In Kim's attempt to reunify the peninsula through military force, he received considerable numbers of men, arms, and equipment from both Moscow and Beijing.[75]

Different factions used the 1950-1953 Korean War as an opportunity to undermine each other. Kim relied heavily on his partisan faction — the close knit group of some 300 guerrilla fighters who had served together in Manchuria.[76] The domestic faction, which hailed from South Korea, was blamed for the military setbacks and political failure to unify the peninsula. The indigenous Korean communist group was accused of plotting a coup against Kim Il Sung during the Korean War. Twelve individuals were charged in July 1953 and convicted the following month. Ten of them were sentenced to death, with the remaining two receiving long prison terms. The purported instigator, Pak Hon Yong, was not put on trial until after the war in 1955, sentenced to death, and then executed.[77] Kim also loosened ties with the Soviet Union and gradually weakened the power of the Soviet Korean Faction by purging its senior leader, Ho Kai, although he retained other members of the group. Ho was expelled from the KWP in November 1951, and reportedly committed suicide in August 1953.[78] By 1958 Kim had purged the leadership of the so-called Yanan Faction (including senior leader Kim Tu Bong) composed of those who had worked or fought with the Chinese Communist Party or its military forces.[79]

As a result of these successive purges, by time of the KWP's Fourth Party Congress, held in September 1961, Kim Il Sung had become the absolute dictator of North Korea. According to Kim Il Sung's biographer, Dae-sook Suh: "His [Kim's] long struggle to consolidate power was complete. . . . There were no longer any factions to challenge his position, and for the first time no foreign armed forces were occupying the North."[80] In the process, Kim played up the nationalist freedom fighter credentials of his own faction of the communist movement and conveniently minimized the varied backgrounds and noteworthy contributions of other factions and leaders. Kim also ignored or downplayed the contributions of the Soviet Union and China prior to and during the Korean War. Through a process of complete "indigenization," the Pyongyang regime became an entity autonomous of both Moscow and Beijing. Save for the first years of occupation by the Red Army, North Korea could never be accurately described as a "Soviet satellite" the way many of the countries of East Europe were.[81] North Korean history books were written in such a way as to completely ignore the liberation of northern Korea by the Soviet Red Army and its installation of the regime.

KWP congresses and plenums became less and less frequent, and their deliberations less and less substantive. Part of the reason for the "subservience" of the delegates appears to be the significant turnover between congresses: between 41 and 72 percent of the members of Central Committees selected at each party congress were new to their positions.[82] The last full party congress to be held when Kim Il Sung was alive was in 1980. Significantly, the main purpose of Sixth Party Congress appeared to have been to give clear but veiled notice to the KWP membership of Kim Jong Il's status as his father's heir. The son was appointed to the Politburo, its Presidium, and he became the second ranking member of the party's Military Commission.[83]

Is the Party Over? Indeed, no new party congress has been held since Kim Il Sung's death. Since a congress has not occurred in 35 years and other KWP meetings seem to be few and far between, the question must be asked whether the party has ceased to be the leading organization in North Korea. While the KWP may no longer be the dominant organizational entity in North Korea, it is certainly not irrelevant (although the Party Congress appears to be dormant — see Figure 2). Part of the explanation may lie in a dictator's efforts to play bureaucratic games to keep the reins of power concentrated in his hands and ensure no challenger emerges. Many dictators have shifted the prime bureaucratic entity through which they exert control and rule of their country to avoid power accumulating in any one place. Moreover, in totalitarian regimes, this shift may be pursued because of the need to reenergize the system by focusing on what is perceived to be a more dynamic bureaucracy. Then, in the 1970s, for example, Kim Il Sung appears to have shifted his focus for ruling North Korea from the party to the state apparatus.[84] Similarly, at various times Kim the father and Kim the son have chosen to emphasize the role of the military at the expense of the party and the state bureaucracies: in the 1960s, Kim Il Sung increased the power of the KPA; then in the late 1990s, Kim Jong Il raised the profile of the military again.[85] China's Mao Zedong tried similar moves during the Cultural Revolution, turning to students to reenergize the Chinese Communist Party. Then, in the late 1960s, when the youthful Red Guards proved uncontrollable and unruly, Mao turned to the armed forces to restore order and run the country.

Since his father's death, Kim Jong Il appears to have relied more on other bureaucratic organs and organizations, most notably the National Defense Commission and the KPA. These organizations will be discussed briefly below in the "Coercive Apparatus" section and in greater detail in a subsequent monograph. This raises a question: Why did the Kims (father and son) find it more convenient to circumvent the KWP? The Elder Kim may simply have found it too bothersome and irrelevant to the business of ruling North Korea. The Younger Kim may have drawn the same conclusion. But there might be more to it than this as far as Kim Jong Il is concerned. From the 1960s until Kim Il Sung's death, there does not appear to have been much discernible dissent or autonomous activity. In the era of Kim Jong Il, however, at least some limited dissent or autonomous society activity has emerged. This is relatively modest at the elite and mass levels. Within the regime itself, there appears to be some degree of dissent, but these accounts are sketchy, unreliable, and impossible to confirm. The best evidence of actual elite dissent is the defections of the past decade or so. However, many of these defectors flee to escape imminent punishment for misdeeds, or because they believe they have fallen from favor and are about to be purged. Ordinary North Koreans have engaged in sporadic dissent expressed in leaflets, posters, and orally in at least some areas of the country.[86] It is possible that one reason behind the younger Kim's preference for not ruling directly through the KWP bureaucracy is that there is some degree of questioning of or quibbling with the younger Kim from the "party faithful," or at least that Kim believes this might be so.

Things have changed since the early 1990s: defections of elite and ordinary North Koreans have risen significantly. In the 1990s, defections to South Korea hovered around 100 per year, but by 2000 and 2001 the numbers of defectors had shot up into the hundreds.[87] The most senior defector was Hwang Jong Yop, who was a key advisor and interpreter of ideology; other senior officials included both diplomats and soldiers.

The party and its nucleus of elites remains a sizeable and significant entity that Kim cannot ignore. A total KWP membership of some three million – dominated by an apparatchik elite numbering approximately several hundred thousand – support the system because they directly owe their jobs, status, and livelihood to the perpetuation of the regime. With the regime's demise, they would lose their power, privilege, and hence be unable to provide for their families. As one defector told journalist and author Bradley Martin: "In my case, if you asked for one big reason I defected, I would answer: Beijing exposed me to unlimiited [sic] outside information. I realized that if unification came, it would be by North Korean collapse or absorption into South Korea, I would become unemployed. . . ."[88] Moreover, fear of retribution or persecution for crimes and misdeeds by the regime must be high among elites. The fear that they will be held accountable for the torture and executions, not to mention other horrors that will only come to light after the regime collapses, is understandable and serves as a powerful motivator to maintain their support for the regime.[89] To sum up, most elites continue to see their fates as being intertwined with that of the regime. If these elites did start to waver, then the regime would be in very serious trouble.

Some analysts and observers claim that Kim Jong Il's power is not absolute and identify the existence of various factions or bureaucratic groupings. Some, such as Selig Harrison, insist there are hardliners and reformers;[90] others, notably Daniel Pinkston, discuss differences based upon presumed institutional interests and talk about "bureaucratic stakeholders."[91] Certainly, this is what North Korean officials from Kim Jong Il on down tell foreign interlocutors. But other respected analysts discern no evidence of significant pluralism.

One should ask why Kim and other officials feel the need to tell foreigners about the existence of internal opinion or bureaucratic interest groups. They could be telling the truth, or they could be trying to deliberately mislead. In either case, what would be the benefit of "revealing" this information to foreigners? If it is true, it helps them to account for the zigs and zags or contradictory impulses that

Pyongyang exhibits. If it is disinformation, it serves as a convenient way for these officials to justify Pyongyang's hardline, adamant, and the jerky progress on reform and other issues. It allows leaders from Kim Jong Il on down to do what they feel they must do while blaming others. In short, Kim and other savvy officials who meet with foreigners get to avoid being seen as the bad guys. But whatever the truth of the matter — and it probably lies somewhere in between — what these tales of differences of opinion within Pyongyang's elite circles suggest to this writer is that the structure of power may be changing.

Why do I speculate along these lines? In most communist regimes, officials tend to insist that there is complete unity within the party even when there is obviously not. It is important in communist political cultures to maintain the outward appearance of unity even if this is fiction. Of course, these North Korean tales of Pyongyang opinion groupings are not broadcast in official public pronouncements but rather in informal and ostensibly off-the-record conversations between elites and foreign leaders and interlocutors. But the fact that these leaders feel the need to say this in any venue suggests this contains elements of truth as well as elements of a convenient excuse. Of course, the answer could be more straightforward: it might be part of a disinformation campaign.[92]

While there is probably some nascent interest group activity in North Korea, it is unclear the extent to which this is manifest: if this takes the shape of factions that form around particular individuals; kinship constellations; opinion groupings, overt or otherwise; and/or loose groupings of former classmates or army buddies, for example. Albright relates that Kim told her there was a "fifty-fifty" split within the military over whether or not to improve relations with the United States. as well as opposition from within the Ministry of Foreign Affairs.[93]

The bottom line is that everyone who dabbles in the study of North Korean elite politics is engaged in speculation. But under the circumstances, informed speculation is a necessary evil. If factions or opinion groupings are present in Pyongyang, they would seem to be quite limited. Thus, Adrian Buzo's assessment of 6 years ago still seems apropos in North Korea today: "There is no evidence to suggest that competitive factional activity, whether based on sectoral, policy, or personality grounds, has been significant under the Kimist personal autocracies."[94] If it were otherwise, significant elite defections would probably not be occurring. That these defections are happening indicates that senior officials have concluded that the current political environment does not allow for open dissent or debate about policy direction. Instead of feeling able to speak up and "voice" their opinions, these elites are choosing the "exit" option.[95] According to Hwang Jong Yop: ". . . [A]s a dictator he [Kim] has excellent ability. He can organize people so they can't move, can't do anything, and he can keep them under his ideology. As far as I know, the present North Korean dictatorial system is the most precise and thorough in history."[96]

Monopolistic Control of the Coercive Apparatus.

Under Kim Il Sung, the coercive apparatus was extremely effective, and by the 1960s completely under the control of the dictator. Kim could purge at will those individuals deemed disloyal, their families, and their networks of supporters. The coercive apparatus comprises not just the military, but the militia, public security (police), secret police, courts, and system of gulags. Reportedly, "the Ministry of Internal Affairs was by far the largest of the government departments in the DPRK."[97]

The new Korean communist state established in the late 1940s in Pyongyang set about establishing what Charles Armstrong called a "regime of surveillance."[98] This included a massive network of informants. The result was not only a coercive apparatus that was able to penetrate virtually all spheres of society, but a populace who were convinced that "Big Brother" was watching them constantly. According to a defector in the early 1950s: "Where ever there were more than two people gathered there was sure to be a spy."[99] But 50 years later, in the first decade of the 21st century, according to Oh and Hassig, "[t]he surveillance system is not perfect." Nevertheless, these researchers contend that, "for the most part, the system works well."[100]

Kim Jong Il has done everything he can to ensure elite loyalty, especially the allegiance of the KPA. Kim buys the loyalty of top officers with gifts of luxury cars and apartments.[101] The "military first" policy, first declared in 1997, indicates that Kim recognizes where his most critical base of support lies. It appears that the most important entity in North Korea is no longer the KWP but rather the KPA. And Kim's most important position seems to be not leader of the KWP but chair of National Defense Commission.

Nevertheless, while the coercive apparatus appears to be loyal to the regime, its allegiance to Kim Jong Il as an individual may not be as rock solid as it was to his father. There have been defections from this apparatus. Soldiers in particular appear to be extremely loyal by most accounts, including those by defectors. The most dedicated troops are those in Kim's bodyguard which reportedly number in the tens of thousands.[102] However, the strength of their loyalty appears to vary within the armed forces. There have been defections, including some by senior military officers. There have also been rumors of mutinies.[103]

Totalist Ideology.

In North Korea the common dimensions of a totalitarian ideology are reinforced by three distinct Korean elements of the ideology: triumphal survivalism, an ancestor cult, and wounded ultra-nationalism.

Totalitarian regimes espouse totalist ideologies that seem to transform a society and people. The regime has an ambitious program to remake man and society. This is usually articulated in the ideology, and the regime aggressively undertakes to achieve these ambitious goals through mass mobilization of the society. Such efforts at mass mobilization are recognizable to students of Hitler's Germany, Stalin's Soviet Union, Mao's China, and Pol Pot's Cambodia (Kampuchea). However, according to two experts, no other regime has "placed so much emphasis on the politics of mass mobilization" as North Korea.[104]

The regime quickly established mass organizations for peasants, workers, women, and youth.[105] Moreover, one should not overlook the prime example of the armed forces as a "mass organization" and the most readily mobilized entity of all. Mass mobilization campaigns characterized the 1950s and 1960s, and the pattern was only repeated in the 1970s, 1980s, and 1990s for key projects.[106] The

DPRK continues to emphasize mobilization in the 21st century as it pursues policy goals. To improve the prospects for the 2005 harvest, for example, in May and June the regime drafted hundreds of thousands of urban residents to go to the countryside and work on irrigation projects and assist with rice transplanting.[107] Similar efforts take place each year, but the number of people mobilized in 2005 appears to be greater than in recent years. This mobilization is accomplished through organizations that isolate them from their families and inculcate them with regime beliefs and values. From a very early age, children are separated from their parents for extended periods of time: placed in day nurseries or work week nurseries.[108] While at the nursery or school, or in the Young Pioneers or League of Socialist Working Youth activities, or later in military service (for periods as long as 10 years, during which time the many inductees rarely, if ever, get back home to see their families), children and young people spend prolonged periods under regime supervision where they are taught to believe that they owe everything to Kim Il Sung and are indoctrinated with the regime's ideology.[109]

Communist ideology aims to work towards the ultimate goals of global revolution, a classless society, and remaking human nature. But more immediate attention focuses on strengthening the regime through indoctrinating and controlling the "people," closely monitoring those of questionable background and purging "enemies of the people." To these ends, the population is divided into classes (*songbun*): a "core class" of staunch regime supporters, a "wavering class" of unreliables, and a "hostile class" of regime opponents.[110] Those purged are either executed or sent to prisons or labor camps.

Triumphal Survivalism. This element is not unique to Korean communism but exists in especially virulent form on the northern portion of the peninsula. There is a firm belief that the movement has succeeded by triumphing against all odds and that this will continue. The leaders of the movement have led the chosen, and together they have overcome seemingly insurmountable barriers. No hardship is too much whether it be battling Japanese occupiers, American invaders, or prolonged economic deprivations (what Pyongyang cryptically refers to as the "arduous march"). Man makes his own fate, and the dedicated individual will triumph.[111] This is intimately linked to the guerrilla tradition that reinforces this survivalist mentality and underscores the harsh reality that self-reliance and military might are the keys to survival. According to Charles Armstrong: "[t]he attitudes formed out of the guerrilla experience have profoundly influenced North Korean politics to this day. Half a century later, North Korea was still being led by men who were fundamentally shaped by the harsh environment of anti-Japanese struggle in Manchuria."[112] The movement cannot depend on any outside power or entity, and the only reliable guarantees for survival are to possess adequate weaponry to defend oneself.[113] No outsider can be completely trusted, and the assumption, or at least strong suspicion, is that everyone is out to get them. In short, a siege mentality is pervasive.[114]

Dead Emperor's Society. Pyongyang's ideology is "neo-traditionalist" in several aspects: it is backward looking rather than forward looking, focuses on reverence for and obedience to elders and superiors, and makes the supreme leader the personification of the nation.[115] The focus is on a nation-wide cult of the ancestor — the deceased patriarch, the founder of the dynasty: Kim Il Sung. Reverence for the departed leader is made synonymous with the loyalty to the current leader (his son) and the cause of nationalism. There is a consuming focus on building, maintaining, and worshiping portraits, monuments, and edifices to the departed leader. And all current national projects are followed to glorify his legacy. The calendar is replete with remembering and celebrating the past: Kim Il Sung's birthday (April 15) and anniversaries of the founding of the party (October 10), the army (February 8), National Day (September 9), and major accomplishments of the regime. For example, on October 10, 2005, North Korea focused much attention toward celebrating the 60th anniversary of the founding of the KWP.

The reverence for the deceased leader is a latter day form of traditional (Confucian) ancestor worship focused around a cult of the founding emperor of the dynasty.[116] Kim Il Sung's birthday — April 15 — is celebrated every year. Moreover, starting in the mid-1990s, the years were renumbered to commemorate the year of the Kim dynasty. For example, 2006 is *Juche Year* 95. There are heavy religious overtones in the rituals and ceremony that come with it. Kim Jong Il gains legitimacy by being seen to do his filial duty to follow through on the wishes of his deceased father on issues such as unification. He also probably strongly believes that he is dutifully implementing his father's wishes.[117]

Kim Il Sung is depicted as personifying the revolutionary struggle of the Korean people for independence, unification, and respect.[118] The message drummed home is: Kim and his son are synonymous with the people. The ideology has some strong corporeal overtones: the leader is brain or head on the body of the nation, and people are other organs. The body cannot live or function without the brain. Therefore, without the Kim family, there would be no past, no present, and certainly no future.

As a result of this ideological indoctrination, North Korea is home to probably the most oppressive personality cult in the world.[119] Kim Jong Il's legitimacy derived directly from his status as the son of Kim Il Sung, as being the greatest disciple of his father and the twin ideologies of Kim Il Sungism and *Juche*. Everyone wears Kim Il Sung lapel pins, and his portrait is everywhere. There are also statues and shrines, including the ancestral home in Mangyongdae. Songs and poems glorify him. North Koreans of all ages spend hours studying his life and teachings. According to Helen-Louise Hunter: "The most distinguishing feature about the Kim Cult, then, is not its more extreme outward manifestations . . . but the intensity of the people's feelings." There may be "contrived displays of emotions and feigned dedication" in North Korea, but "the overwhelming evidence" suggests a very real and "strong emotional attachment to Kim [Il Sung]."[120]

Indeed, the regime relies so heavily on the Kim family for its legitimacy that it is difficult to imagine the existing system surviving a renunciation of Kim Il Sung and/or the toppling of Kim Jong Il. Pyongyang's civilian and military elites almost certainly consider major change unthinkable if they are to retain their positions of power and privilege. Indoctrination stresses the centrality of the family as a unique "revolutionary" multi-generational clan whose patriotism and heroic exploits date back to 1866 against the U.S. vessel *General Sherman*.[121] This aspect is acknowledged by experts who label North Korea as a "Kimist system" or the "Kim Family Regime."[122]

Wounded Ultra-Nationalism. The third component of North Korea's ideology is a deeply scarred extreme nationalism. Koreans are very much influenced by centuries of being mercilessly exploited by great powers, and by dint of geography serving as a battleground or invasion route for surrounding states. A history of invasion and oppression by China, Japan, and, more recently, by devastation wrought by the U.S. military during the Korean War, has combined to make the Pyongyang regime obsessed with righting the indignities suffered by the Korean people. The "never again" mantra of the Jewish Diaspora, when seeking to move beyond the horror of the Holocaust, would find significant resonance with many Korean inhabitants, both north and south of the Demilitarized Zone (DMZ). In contrast, however, while the Jews have a homeland within the borders of a single state, the ancestral Korean homeland remains politically divided. Because of this history and the unresolved matter of unification, Koreans are ultra-sensitive toward perceived slights and insults to their national pride. While Pyongyang's periodic insistence that the statements of foreign leaders or officials that disparage the regime have "hurt the feelings" of the North Korean people provides useful fodder for propaganda and convenient excuses for postponing talks, this rhetoric may also reflect wounded nationalism.

In this context, the propaganda display arranged for the visiting U.S. Secretary of State in 2000, described by Albright as resembling "an Olympics opening ceremony on steroids,"[123] becomes more comprehensible. The purpose of the elaborately choreographed display was not only to glorify the regime and feed the ego of its supreme dictator, but also to stress the power and resolve of the North Korean people in the face of a hostile and dangerous world. Nevertheless, it is possible that Kim wanted to stage an entertaining and memorable performance for his guest and did not necessarily intend to hammer home a particular message—there was simply no time to come up with a new program.[124] This becomes quite a plausible explanation if one recognizes that North Korea does not have much that can impress foreign dignitaries. Other than displays of actual military power—conventional or WMD—what else, beyond examples of mass mobilization and synchronization, does Kim have to offer?

This wounded nationalism is encapsulated in the ideology of *Juche*. Usually translated as "self-reliance," it is better understood as "self-determination." Many analysts and observers are hard pressed to understand what it really means—how to define it and explain it.

As a result, many end up either getting frustrated and/or claiming it is simply mindless mumbo jumbo that the regime finds useful to cover up its contradictions and inconsistencies. To better appreciate *Juche*, it might be best viewed, as Bruce Cumings suggests, as "a state of mind." Cumings elaborates: "The term literally means being subjective where Korean matters are concerned, putting Korea first in everything."[125] The term, Cumings contends, is "untranslatable." Given wounded Korean nationalism and these insights, perhaps *Juche* is best defined as putting "Korea first (in everything)."[126]

It is not clear to what extent that this ideology of socialism, combined with triumphal survivalism, ancestor worship, and wounded ultra-nationalism, has been undermined by foreign and/or economic crises.

Information Control.

Totalitarian regimes seek to exercise total control over information and all forms of media. Through this control, they can engage in brainwashing or indoctrination on a mass scale. In the era of Kim Il Sung, this control was far easier to enforce than it is in the era of Kim Jong Il. Rapid advances in information technology have made it far more challenging for a totalitarian regime to seal off its population from external sources of information. Nevertheless, under the circumstances, Pyongyang has done a credible job of keeping most people almost completely reliant on the official North Korean media for information and suspicion of any outside propaganda from the United States or South Korea.

Televisions and radio sets in North Korean households are fixed so that they can only receive one approved station, and most people have no access to external print media. But even if they get access to South Korean or Chinese newspapers and magazines, their ability to read these materials is hampered.[127] While the North Korean populace has a high rate of basic literacy with at least 7 years of education, many cannot read Chinese characters, only the indigenous Hangul syllabary.[128] Decades ago Pyongyang purged its writing system of Chinese characters that are still used in South Korean and Japanese publications.[129]

Prior to the 1990s, North Korea was quite tightly sealed off from information about and exposure to the outside world. The emergence of a severe food crisis in North Korea in the early 1990s triggered a massive human flow back and forth across the North Korea-China border. This enabled as many as hundreds of thousands of North Koreans to get firsthand information about and experience with the outside world that may have conflicted with or contradicted information they had received from official North Korean sources.[130] Before this, most ordinary citizens of the DPRK had no opportunity to go abroad except as contract manual laborers in places such as logging camps in the Russian Far East.[131] Otherwise, travel or temporary residence abroad was restricted to elites such as diplomats or soldiers serving as advisors or body guards to Third World dictators.

In addition to the back and forth to China, there has been some tightly controlled interaction with relatives from South Korea for a small number of DPRK citizens, as well as limited exposure to foreign tourists. Also potentially significant has been extended exposure in recent years to foreign aid workers who were able to visit significant areas of North Korea, sometimes unescorted.[132]

We know that there has been increased use of cellular telephones and viewing of video cassettes in North Korea in the past several years. Perhaps thousands of cell phones are now in use. These are used mainly to conduct business along the border with China, but they also permit communication between family members in North Korea and those in China and South Korea. According to one estimate, "about one-third of the defectors in South Korea regularly talk to family members back in North Korea."[133] Video cassette tapes are smuggled in from South Korea and played on video cassette recorders (VCRs) bought on the black market in China. As a result, North Koreas are watching bootleg tapes of South Korean soap operas that show the prosperity and modernity south of the DMZ. These tapes have reportedly spread across North Korea, whereas cell phones only work in certain parts of the country.[134]

These developments certainly have the potential to undermine complete regime control of information, and Pyongyang has taken these developments extremely seriously.[135] There have been periodic crackdowns on both cell phone usage and illicit video viewings.

For example, following the mysterious explosion at a train yard in Ryongchon on the main rail line between Pyongyang and Beijing on April 22, 2004, the regime severely curtailed cell phone use and more closely monitored wireless communications.[136] Although there is no evidence that this was anything but an accidental explosion of chemical fertilizer, it appears that the regime believed this could have been an assassination attempt on Kim Jong Il whose train traveled through the station 8 hours earlier on a return trip from China. There was concern that cell phones may have been used to plan the incident and/or even detonate the explosion. As of early 2005, frequency blocking devices have also been activated in cities near the border with China, and executions of cell phone users have been reported.[137]

The regime is alarmed over the proliferation of illicit videos and the fads they spawn in South Korean slang, fashions (including hairstyles), and goods.[138] Tactics used by the regime include surrounding a neighborhood one evening, shutting off the power, and then going dwelling to dwelling to see what tape is lodged inside the VCR.[139] We also know that there is clandestine listening to foreign radio broadcasts from South Korea and Voice of America by some in North Korea.[140]

Social scientists refer to a dynamic called the "spiral of silence" that is operative in environments such as North Korea where there is strict control of information and heavy indoctrination reinforced by people's fear of the consequences of publicly challenging or questioning the official line.[141] In such a situation, a person thinks that he or she is the only person who has doubts and feels guilty, unpatriotic, or deviant. Such are the results of "brainwashing." Because no one else expresses similar feelings, the person believes he/she is alone in feeling this way. As a result of this (as well as out of a fear of being punished for having bad thoughts), the individual remains silent or shares their doubts with perhaps one other highly trusted friend or loved one.

However, once someone speaks out publicly with their doubts or criticism, the spiral of silence is broken and others realize there are not alone their supposed heterodox thoughts. Once the spiral is broken, the system can begin to unravel fairly quickly with dramatic results. The results can be especially dramatic once people realize they can escape punishment for speaking out, and there is safety in numbers: suddenly the regime is seriously threatened, such as in China in 1989, or can even collapse as in the revolutions of 1989 in Eastern Europe. Perhaps the most shocking illustration of the end of the spiral silence is in Romania in December 1989. It began with a small group of hecklers booing at a Bucharest rally where Nicolae Ceausescu was speaking which was being broadcast live on December 21, 1989. The heckling quickly snowballed, and a day later Ceausescu and his wife were arrested and executed a few days afterwards.[142]

Condition of Terror.

One characteristic in the mindset of leaders in totalitarian regimes is that they tend to be extremely paranoid. Because of their experiences in the conspiratorial activities involved in the business of making revolution (i.e., seizing and holding power), they are intimately familiar with how schemers and putchists operate and are overly sensitized to potential threats. They tend to assume all rhetoric or activity even vaguely critical is directed at undermining or overthrowing the regime, even when elites or ordinary people express legitimate grievances or frustration with no intention beyond resolving their specific issue. Moreover, even if the protests are judged to be relatively harmless, they are usually ruthlessly suppressed for fear that they might inspire others. The automatic response to dissent is a swift iron fist to make an example of the perpetrators and to send the message that such actions will not be tolerated. These examples and the presumption that a contemplated act of protest or dissent will be crushed immediately instill a climate of fear as people become apprehensive of a knock at the door in the middle of the night. Fear becomes so pervasive that people believe that the authorities see and hear everything: the perception that "Big Brother" *is* watching you.[143]

In addition, people fear for the consequences of what one person's perceived misdeed might hold for a whole family. Purges in North Korea involve not just an individual but his or her entire family being sent to the gulag. The result is a major deterrent to wrongdoing because of the knowledge that the punishment will not just be inflicted on the individual but upon his/her extended family.[144] The climate of terror is instilled not just by the visible elements of the coercive apparatus — the public security bureau, the military, and the courts — but also by a fear of being informed on by a colleague, a friend, or even a loved one.[145]

The climate of terror is still quite pervasive in 21st century North Korea, although it has weakened to the extent that it has not dissuaded hundreds of thousands from traveling to China and thousands from attempting to defect to South Korea via a third country (usually China). The motivations appear to be the harshness of economic conditions in the country of the past 2 decades or fear of continued persecution among those marked for life as troublemakers or unreliables. This is the primary reason given by Kang Chol Hwan for his defection as recounted in his memoirs, *The Aquariums of Pyongyang*. Kang knew that he was under surveillance and concluded that it was only a matter of time before he was rearrested and sent back to the gulag.

Nevertheless, the climate of fear in North Korea has weakened to the extent that bribery and corruption are all pervasive. Functionaries and officials readily accept bribes to dispense goods, issue documents, and tolerate travel without permits. And regime informants, border guards, and train conductors routinely accept bribes to look the other way.[146] There are also reports that the punishment of one's entire family for the transgressions of one member may now be less draconian.[147]

Centralized Economy.

In a totalitarian state, the regime attempts to control most, if not all, economic activity. In communist variants of totalitarianism, central planning is deemed essential to ensure rapid and coordinated economic development. Normally this entails multiyear plans (usually in increments of 5 years). Central planners decide what is to be produced, the quantity, and the price. All major commodities and foodstuffs are allocated by the state. Most basic necessities and highly desirable goods, including food and consumer items tend to be rationed and distributed through a network of the regime. The result is that individuals come to depend on the regime for most daily necessities. Often the system does not provide enough goods to satisfy demand. An unpredictable supply of goods leads people to hoard items as a precaution. The Centrally Planned Economy (CPE) and the rational reaction of consumers virtually guarantee that demand will outstrip supply. Therefore economist Janos Kornai has dubbed the system "the shortage economy."[148] Because of the inefficiencies and bottlenecks inherent in the system, an informal or "second" economy (aka "black market") develops to satisfy people's wants. The result is corruption or what communist regimes tend to call "economic crimes."

A CPE emerged in North Korea in March 1946 with the establishment of an "economic planning bureau." Within 12 months (February 1947), a "National Economic Rehabilitation and Development" blueprint had been adopted.[149] In the era of Kim Il Sung, the CPE certainly was not perfect, but it did function reasonably well to the extent that North Korea enjoyed respectable economic growth, and DPRK citizens enjoyed a decent standard of living. By the 1960s, North Koreans actually may have had a better standard of living than their South Korean cousins. And the central planning bureaucrats in Pyongyang appear to have been more successful than their counterparts in other communist states at collectivizing agriculture without precipitating famine. The economic system, while it experienced increasing problems in the 1970s and 1980s, could count on loans and subsidized fuel and other assistance from fraternal socialist states to mitigate the impact of these.

By the 1990s, however, in the final years of Kim Il Sung's life, these loans and subsidies dried up, and Moscow and other capitals insisted that Pyongyang pay with hard currency for trade items. In the mid-1990s, as food situation became more desperate, people began to migrate in search of food. Hunger and malnourishment became starvation. The famine dramatically demonstrated the weakening of the regime: the breakdown of its food distribution system. In other words, the regime proved unable to ensure its populace was fed, and people had to adopt survival strategies by relying on their own initiative and ingenuity.[150] However, food aid from overseas is depicted as a gift—the manifestation of a latter-day tribute system whereby Kim Jong Il receives offerings from afar as tokens of the esteemed and exalted status in which he is held in the world.

What were the causes of the famine and how can one assess its impact? There is actually widespread consensus among experts about the causes. But, it is worthwhile to note that North Korean agriculture is quite impressive in a number of respects. First, collectivization was achieved in the late 1950s without triggering the kind of major famine that the same process did in places such as the former Soviet Union and China.[151] Moreover, North Korea is a highly urbanized and industrial country, with only approximately one-third of its populace being engaged in full-time agriculture.[152]

Having said this, the impact of the collapse of communism in Eastern Europe and the Soviet Union (1989-91) that resulted in the swift and sudden dismantlement of Pyongyang's economic support network made a major crisis in North Korean agriculture inevitable. The DPRK heavily relied on subsidized inputs, especially petroleum, to operate its entire economy. But the end of this support hit the agricultural sector especially hard. North Korea's agriculture suffers from many of the same systemic distortions and inefficiencies as other communist countries where the agrarian sector has been collectivized. The choice of crops and farming techniques is often not appropriate to the soil, topography, or climatic conditions. The results are poor yields, depleted soil, and serious land erosion. In addition, agriculture is "input intensive," requiring large amounts of fuel, fertilizer, and equipment to keep it functioning. Virtually all aspects are highly mechanized and depend on chemical fertilizer, and this requires a constant infusion of energy resources. Since North Korea is not an oil producer, it depends totally on imported petroleum to power tractors, irrigation pumps, and factories producing chemical fertilizer. Certainly coal is mined domestically and can be used for some of the DPRK's energy needs, but oil seems indispensable.[153]

The famine was exacerbated by severe weather and flooding, but the situation became chronic because the regime refused to institute systemic changes or reform. Instead, Pyongyang looked to foreign governments and nongovernment organizations (NGOs) to provide famine relief. Starting in 1995, the regime adopted an explicit aid-based strategy, and the following year a variety of NGOs were permitted to operate in the country. Significantly, for the most part, the regime took responsibility for distributing the aid through its own Public Distribution System (PDS).[154]

But rumors of the complete and irreversible collapse of the regime appear to have been greatly exaggerated. In late 2005 Pyongyang appeared to be reactivating its PDS.[155] The famine appears to be ameliorated significantly although not completely resolved. But the regime insisted that the country has recovered from the famine, and there is no more need for food aid. They claimed that the country enjoyed a "bumper harvest." Thus, the regime announced that by the end of 2005 all foreign aid organizations must cease their food aid projects in the country. Instead the effort should be focused on development assistance.[156] But it is not clear whether all aid groups would be forced out, especially if they officially switch from food aid to development assistance.[157]

Why did the regime take this step? First, it is very likely that the regime wanted to reassert control over the country. Second, the regime wanted foreign aid workers out of the country. They are viewed as negative and possible dangerous influences on the people of North Korea. The regime wants to avoid the perception among the people that the country depends on foreign assistance.[158] Third, the food situation has improved considerably although problems abound, including widespread malnutrition. According to United Nations (UN) estimates, 7 percent of North Koreans are still starving, and more than one-third of the populace is "chronically malnourished."[159] The regime may be confident that agriculture is on the mend. Whether this is so, Pyongyang is now receiving considerable aid from China and South Korea, assistance that comes without many restrictions, or controls, or intrusive foreign personnel. This kind of hands-off aid from neighbors is much preferred to that provided by meddlesome Western NGOs and relief agencies.

To sum up, North Korea's CPE is still in place and functioning. While the famine has proved highly challenging to the regime, its performance and response are not so different to those of CPEs in other communist regimes. The distortions and inefficiencies could be compensated for and/or overlooked until the collapse of Soviet bloc aid in the late 1980s. This dealt a body blow to Pyongyang's economy generally, and in particular savaged its "input-intensive" agricultural sector. The response to the famine this triggered was not systemic reform or even serious introspection, but ad hoc efforts to mitigate the disaster through foreign aid and reform around the edges. The latter adaptations included tolerating private food markets and raising prices.[160]

CONCLUSION

North Korea is an eroding totalitarian regime that has existed for approximately 4 decades. While totalitarianism is a powerful and intimidating system, it places tremendous strain on a state and a society — demanding constant activity and mobilization of personnel and exploitation of resources. The costs of maintaining heightened ideological indoctrination, an ever-vigilant coercive apparatus, and a large national defense organization are high and ultimately debilitating. To maintain these for decades results in fatigue and burnout.[161] Eventually leaders and followers reach a point where both are physically and mentally exhausted, and the country's infrastructure and resources become devastated. North Korea's elite and ordinary people appear to be approaching this point. But this fatigue and burnout does not appear to produce much in the way of protest or dissent, let alone revolt; most likely the majority of people in North Korea are simply too tired to do much more than focus their time and energy on providing the basic necessities for their families and a few of life's luxuries for special occasions.

While the regime is still ruled by an absolute dictator who leads a ruling party-military-state with a continued monopoly of the coercive apparatus, there has been some slippage in the first of these areas and other features have eroded noticeably. First, Kim Jong Il, although virtually an absolute dictator, appears to take into account the opinions of others the way his father did not. And ideology no longer appears to be so focused on transforming the state and society and more on the instrumental goals of economic recovery, development, and firming up regime power. While a condition of terror remains palpable, it is no longer all pervasive, and individuals are able to navigate or circumvent the system without fearing that they face dire consequences. As a result of the shift in ideology and alleviation of climate of terror, the regime has become "corrupted" — literally as bribery is rampant, and figuratively as the Leninist regime, what Ken Jowitt would characterize as "neo-traditionalist."[162] Meanwhile, the Stalinist centrally planned economy has been eroded seriously, and the monopoly of mass communication has loosened significantly. The regime has attempted to repair the latter two elements, but it is not clear to what extent this will be successful.

The regime appears to be stable and not on the brink of collapse. While it is difficult to speculate about the longevity of North Korea as a political entity, it is more manageable to forecast the future of totalitarianism in the DPRK. Totalitarian regimes rarely endure longer than several decades and almost never survive the passing of the absolute dictator. In fact, Pyongyang is unique in that it is the only totalitarian regime to have weathered a leadership transition. Indeed, North Korea is the world's "longest lasting totalitarian regime, having spanned some 4 decades and surviving generational leadership succession."[163] While Kim Jong Il's party-military-state faces numerous challenges, perhaps none is more daunting than the succession question. Kim probably has at most 10-15 years in which to pave the way for one of his offspring to succeed him. If he lives long enough, it is possible he could be successful. What is less likely is that totalitarianism could survive another leadership transition.

Perhaps the clearest indication of the status and fate of Pyong-yang's totalitarian regime over the next 10 years or so will come in how the arrangements for the succession to Kim Jong Il are handled. Is there evidence that a particular individual is being groomed to succeed Kim? The answer appears to be "yes."[164] Some other key indicators to monitor are signs of dissent among elites and masses, especially fissures that might occur within the party or military. By carefully charting trends, observers can make it less likely that they will be caught off guard by the actions of North Korea's leader or changes in its political system.

ENDNOTES

1. This is what Selig S. Harrison seems to suggest, but the term is mine. See Harrison's *Korean Endgame: A Strategy for Unification and U.S. Disengagement*, Princeton, NJ: Princeton University Press, 2002.

2. See, for example, on currency counterfeiting: Bill Gertz, "U.S. Accuses North Korea of $100 Bill Counterfeiting," *Washington Times*, October 12, 2005. The article highlights a U.S. Government investigation which concluded that the DPRK has engaged in the counterfeiting of U.S. currency for many years. See, for example on drug trafficking, a report by Raphael F. Perl, *Drug Trafficking and North Korea:*

Issues for U.S. Policy, Washington, DC: Congressional Research Service, December 5, 2003. For a disturbing big picture study of the spectrum of North Korean criminal activity, see David L. Asher, "The North Korean Criminal State, Its Ties to Organized Crime, and the Possibility of WMD Proliferation," posted November 15, 2005, on *www.nautilus.org/for a/security/0592Asher.html.*

3. Interestingly, an ethnic Korean nightclub worker who claimed to have entertained Kim Jong Il's eldest son, Kim Jong Nam, in Tokyo one night remarked that he reminded her of a "Yakuza godfather." See Bradley K. Martin, *Under the Loving Care of the Fatherly Leader: North Korea and Kim Dynasty*, New York: St. Martin's Press, 2004, p. 698.

4. Asher, "The North Korean Criminal State."

5. "'Corporatism' is an ambiguous term." On corporatism, see Douglas Chalmers, "Corporatism and Comparative Politics," in Howard J. Wiarda, ed., *New Directions in Comparative Politics*, Boulder, CO: Westview Press, 1985, pp. 56-79 [the quote is from p. 57]; and Frederick B. Pike and Thomas Stritch, eds., *The New Corporatism: Social and Political Structures in the Iberian World*, South Bend, IN: University of Indiana Press, 1974. On applying the concept to North Korea, see Bruce Cumings, "The Corporate State in North Korea," in Hagen Koo, ed., *State and Society in Contemporary Korea*, Ithaca, NY: Cornell University Press, 1993, pp. 213-246; and Harrison, *Korean Endgame*, pp. 23-24.

6. As mentioned in endnote 1, the term "fragmented totalitarianism" is mine, not Harrison's. Conceptual confusion surrounds Harrison's depiction of North Korea's political system. On the one hand, he refers to it as an "Orwellian totalitarian regime" (pp. xvi, 5), while on the other, he argues there are "reform" and "Old Guard" factions (e.g., p. 25). This suggests a more diffuse distribution of power than that usually associated with totalitarianism. Thus, while the term "fragmented totalitarianism" seems contradictory, it seems the best way to capture how Harrison views the DPRK.

7. On the term as applied to post-Mao China, see Kenneth Lieberthal, *Governing China*, New York: W. W. Norton, 1995.

8. Martin, *Under the Loving Care of the Fatherly Leader*; Kongdan Oh and Ralph C. Hassig, *North Korea Through the Looking Glass*, Washington, DC: Brookings Institution Press, 2000, pp. 35-36, 38.

9. Andrew Scobell, "Making Sense of North Korea: Pyongyang and Comparative Communism," *Asian Security*, Vol. 1, No. 3, forthcoming Winter 2005, pp. 245-266.

10. As Bradley Martin notes: "Pyongyang-watchers who were not blinded by ideological sympathy had known all along . . . that Pyongyang gave full expression to the theory and practice of totalitarianism." See Martin, *Under the Loving Care of the Fatherly Leader*, p. 628. Joel S. Wit, Daniel B. Poneman, and Robert L. Gallucci also characterize the system thus. See their *Going Critical: The First North Korean Nuclear Crisis*, Washington, DC: Brookings Institution Press, 2004, p. 381. For analysts who adopt the totalitarian framework, see Robert Scalapino and Chong

Sik Lee, eds., *Communism in Korea*, 2 vols., Berkeley and Los Angeles, University of California Press, 1972; Helen Louise Hunter, *Kim Il Sung's North Korea*, New York: Praeger, 1999; and Oh and Hassig, *North Korea Through the Looking Glass*.

11. Carl Friedrich and Zibigniew Brzezinski, *Totalitarian Dictatorship and Autocracy*, Cambridge, MA: Harvard University Pres, 1956.

12. Scholars often overlook the "militarized nature of [communist] ... regimes." Scobell, "Making Sense of North Korea," p. 6.

13. *Ibid.*, p. 7.

14. For more discussion of post-totalitarianism, see *Ibid.*, pp. 2-3; and Juan J. Linz, *Totalitarian and Authoritarian Regimes*, Boulder, CO: Lynne Rienner, 2000; originally published in 1975 in Fred I. Greenstein and Nelson W. Polsby, eds., *The Handbook of Political Science*, Vol. 8, Reading, MA: Addison-Wesley, 1975.

15. Richard Lowenthal, "Development Vs. Utopia in Communist Policy," in Chalmers Johnson, ed., *Change in Communist Systems*, Stanford, CA: Stanford University Press, 1970, pp. 33-116.

16. Andrei Lankov, "North Korean Refugees in Northeast China," *Asian Survey*, Vol. XLIV, No. 6, November/December 2004, pp. 856-873.

17. For some of the speculation, see James Brooke, "Where Kim's Portrait Hung in Pyongyang, A Baffling Blankness," *New York Times* (Washington edition), November 18, 2004; Anthony Faiola and Sachiko Sakamaki, "Missing Homages Spur Rumors on N. Korean Deified Leader May Be Shedding Cult Status," *Washington Post*, November 19, 2004; Jasper Becker, "Shifting Signs in North Korea: Kim Jong Il Dials Back Personality Cult as Protest Activities Pick Up," *Christian Science Monitor* December 1, 2004.

18. See the analyst quoted in James Brooke, "Japanese Officials Warn of Fissures in North Korea," *New York Times* (Washington edition), November 22, 2004.

19. Madeleine Albright with Bill Woodward, *Madam Secretary*, New York: Miramax Books, 2003, p. 465.

20. Cited in Oh and Hassig, *North Korea*, p. 91.

21. Some defector accounts suggest otherwise. For example, some suggest conflicts or at least tensions between father and son during at least the elder Kim's final years. See, for example, Martin, *Under the Loving Care of the Fatherly Leader*, pp. 505-507.

22. Dae-Sook Suh, *Kim Il-Sung: The North Korean Leader*, 2nd ed., New York: Columbia University Press, n.d., p. xiv.

23. On showing filial respect, see Michael Breen, *Kim Jong Il: North Korea's Dear Leader*, Singapore: John Wiley and Sons, 2004, p. 46. Others researchers argue that his limited public appearances stem from shyness and "awkwardness around people." Oh and Hassig, *North Korea*, pp. 90, 93-94.

24. The successor's dilemma proved the undoing of at least three anointed successors to Mao Zedong: Liu Shaoqi, Lin Biao, and Deng Xiaoping; and two anointed successors to Deng Xiaoping: Hu Yaobang and Zhao Ziyang. A similar dynamic played out with Hu Jintao's succession to Jiang Zemin, but Hu, like Jiang before him, proved more adept than the above named aspirants at surmounting the successor's dilemma. For discussion of this dilemma as it relates to Hu Jintao, see Murray Scot Tanner, "Hu Jintao as China's Emerging National Security Leader," in Andrew Scobell and Larry Wortzel, eds., *Civil-Military Change in China: Elites, Institutes, and Ideas After the 16th Party Congress*, Carlisle Barracks, PA: U.S. Army War College, Strategic Studies Institute, 2004, pp. 50-51.

25. Suh, *Kim Il-Sung*, p. xv.

26. Breen, *Kim Jong Il*, p. 12.

27. Peter Maass, "The Last Emperor," *New York Times Magazine*, October 19, 2003, pp. 38-47, 60-61, 128-130. For another recent analysis of Kim Jong Il, see Jerrold M. Post, *Leaders and Their Followers in a Dangerous World*, Ithaca, New York: Cornell University Press, 2004, chapter 12.

28. Albright, with Woodward, *Madam Secretary*, pp. 462, 467.

29. For a more detailed analysis of North Korean intentions, see Andrew Scobell, *North Korea's Strategic Intentions*, Carlisle Barracks, PA: U.S. Army War College, Strategic Studies Institute, July 2005.

30. Albright, with Woodward, *Madam Secretary*, p. 465.

31. Andrew Scobell, "North Korea on the Brink: Breakdown or Breakthrough?" in Carolyn Pumphrey, ed., *The Rise of China in Asia*, Carlisle Barracks, PA: U.S. Army War College, Strategic Studies Institute, 2001, p. 213; Breen, *Kim Jong Il*, pp. 45-461; Martin, *Under the Loving Care of the Fatherly Leader*, pp. 648-649.

32. A North Korean defector, former diplomat Ko Young Hwan, while being dismissive of Kim's abilities in many areas, grudgingly acknowledges that he "has some talent in culture and the arts." Martin, *Under the Loving Care of the Fatherly Leader*, p. 510. A South Korean newspaper publisher who dined with Kim for 4 hours in August 2000 described him as "acting more like a Broadway producer with a smash hit on this hands than a dictator running a repressive and impoverished regime." Maass, "The Last Emperor," p. 41.

33. For an account of his movie making activities, see Martin, *Under the Loving Care of the Fatherly Leader*, chapter 13. This chapter also discusses Kim's involvement in musical and theatrical extravaganzas.

34. On his collection of movies, see *Ibid.*, p. 331.

35. Albright, with Woodward, *Madam Secretary*, p. 466-67.

36. Maass, "The Last Emperor."

37. Martin, *Under the Loving Care of the Fatherly Leader*, p. 222.

38. Maass, "The Last Emperor," p. 38.

39. Lewis L. Gould, *The Modern American Presidency*, Lawrence, KS: University Press of Kansas, 2003, pp. 179-190.

40. See, for example, Robert A. Strong, *Working in the World: Jimmy Carter and the Making of American Foreign Policy*, Baton Rouge, LA: Louisiana State University Press, 2000, p. 264. Strong argues that this depiction is unfair, and that Carter's real failing was an "unwillingness to prioritize." *Ibid.*, p. 265. Another scholar contends "Carter envisioned a system where only the president would know the larger picture, and he would make the ultimate decision. In practice that meant that issues large and small flowed toward the Oval Office. The most celebrated case was the degree of Carter's personal involvement over who was allowed to use the White House tennis courts." Gould, *The Modern American Presidency*, p. 184.

41. Gould, *The Modern American Presidency*, pp. 180, 182.

42. Oh and Hassig, *North Korea*, p. 98.

43. Potemkin villages were, purportedly, the facades of model villages built at the order of Russian minister Grigori Aleksandrovich Potemkin to impress Empress Catherine II when she visited Crimea in the late 18th century. A Potemkin village has come to refer to an idyllic construct desired to impress and deceive a visiting dignitary or dignitaries and thus hide a reality that is far from idyllic. Some have suggested that the origins of the term may itself be a kind of "Potemkin" myth and that the Russian minister has gotten an undeserved bad rap.

44. On Mao's experiences with Potemkin villages, see Li Zhisui, *The Private Life of Chairman Mao*, New York: Random House, 1994. On speculation about Kim Il Sung and Potemkin villages, see Martin, *Under the Loving Care of the Fatherly Leader*, pp. 499, 518-519. See also the story of Kim Il Sung related in *ibid.*, p. 503.

45. Oh and Hassig, *North Korea*, pp. 127-133.

46. Martin, *Under the Loving Care of the Fatherly Leader*, pp. 2, and 715, footnote 1. See also Hunter, *Kim Il-sung's North Korea*, chapter 14.

47. "North Korea's Potemkin hospital," *The Economist*, September 12, 1992, p. 37.

48. Oh and Hassig, *North Korea*, p. 192. Of course, the concept was conceived by Herbert Simon.

49. On the extent of his trips prior to 2000, see Oh and Hassig, *North Korea*, pp. 90-91. It is also rumored that Kim spent some time at a military academy in East Germany, but this has not been confirmed.

50. Konstantin Pulikovsky, *Vostochnii Ekspress: Po Rossiis Kim Chen Ilom* [*Orient Express: Across Russia with Kim Jong Il*] Moscow: Gorodets, 2002. The volume was published in Russian. For a synopsis in English, see James Brooke, "A Telling North Korean Journey: Russian Envoy Writes of Riding the Rails with Kim Jong Il," *New York Times* (Washington edition), December 3, 2002.

51. Martin, *Under the Loving Care of the Fatherly Leader*, pp. 319, 649.

52. On movies as an important source of information about foreign countries, see *ibid.*, p. 331.

53. Oh and Hassig, "The New North Korea," in Hassig and Oh, *Korea Briefing*, p. 84.

54. Martin, *Under the Loving Care of the Fatherly Leader*, p. 650.

55. I am indebted to Colonel Dwight Raymond for this important point.

56. Martin, *Under the Loving Care of the Fatherly Leader*, p. 678.

57. *Ibid.*, p. 284.

58. This point is also made by Maass. See "The Last Emperor," 46-47.

59. Oh and Hassig, *North Korea*, p. 97.

60. For the time being, let us leave aside the question of whether North Korea will, indeed, give up its nuclear program as it has pledged to do in Beijing in the Six Party Talks statement of principles in September 2005. This writer believes that it is extremely unlikely that Pyongyang will give it up. See Andrew Scobell and Michael Chambers, "The Fallout of a Nuclear North Korea," *Current History*, Vol. 104, No. 683, September 2005, pp. 289-294.

61. Jerold Post appears to believe that the disorder might prove fatal to Kim. See Post, *Leaders and Their Followers in a Dangerous World*, pp. 255-256.

62. For one informed journalistic account of Kim Jong Il, see Breen, *Kim Jong Il*.

63. For example, Martin, *Under the Loving Care of the Fatherly Leader*, p. 220.

64. Cited in *ibid.*, p. 684. The title of the article was "The Korean Revolution Carried Out From the Son's Generation to the Grandson's Generation."

65. *Ibid.*, p. 679.

66. Oh and Hassig, *North Korea*, pp. 35-36.

67. Scobell, "Making Sense of North Korea," pp. 3, 15-16.

68. For some informed speculation on this issue, see Joo Sang-min, "N. Korea Not Prepared to Announce Successor: Experts," Yonhap News Agency, October 7, 2005; and Martin, *Under the Loving Care of the Fatherly Leader*, Chapter 37.

69. This is according to a story carried in the South Korean newspaper, *Joong Ang Ilbo* (internet version), Seoul, November 25, 2005.

70. Charles K. Armstrong, *The North Korean Revolution, 1945-1950*, Ithaca, NY: Cornell University Press, 2003, p. 108. See also Lee, *Korean Workers' Party*, p. 79. The precise origins and evolution of the Korean communist movement are rather complicated. For a detailed history and analysis, see Scalapino and Lee, *Communism in Korea*; and Chong-Sik Lee, *The Korean Workers' Party: A Short History*.

71. Merle Fainsod and Jerry F. Hough, *How the Soviet Union is Governed*, Cambridge, MA: Harvard University Press, 1979, pp. 144-146, ff.

72. There is disagreement regarding the degree of Soviet control and domination of the Korean communist regime that the Red Army installed. One recent study by Andrei Lankov argues Soviet control was very strong, while another recent study by Charles Armstrong argues that the new regime actually was permitted considerable autonomy. For the fomer interpretation, see Lankov, *From Stalin to Kim Il Sung: The Formation of North Korea, 1945-1960*, New Brunswick, NJ: Rutgers University Press, 2002; for the latter interpretation, see Armstrong, *The North Korean Revolution*, chapter 2.

73. Suh, *Kim Il-Sung*, pp. 102, 107, and 356, note 1. The quote is from note 1 on p. 356.

74. Contrary to popular belief, Kim does not appear to have been handpicked and groomed by the Soviet Union. On this point, Lankov and Armstrong agree. Indeed, Lankov claims Kim became the top leader "almost by accident." Lankov, *From Stalin to Kim Il Sung*, p. 59. See also Armstrong, *The North Korean Revolution*, pp. 39, 55.

75. On Chinese assistance in the lead up to the Korean War, see Chen Jian, *China's Road to the Korean War: The Making of the Sino-American Confrontation*, New York: Columbia University Press, 1994.

76. Kim's biographer concludes that his partisan band comprised no more 300 fighters at most. Suh, *Kim Il-Sung*, p. 38.

77. *Ibid.*, pp. 130-134.

78. *Ibid.*, pp. 123-126.

79. *Ibid.*, pp. 150-154.

80. *Ibid.*, p. 168.

81. "... [D]espite the high degree of Soviet influence and support in constructing a communist-oriented regime in their zone of occupation, communism in North Korea almost immediately became 'indigenized,' and the distinctive Korean elements of the North Korean system were evident from the very beginning of the regime." Armstrong, *The North Korean Revolution*, pp. 3-4.

82. Adrian Buzo, *The Guerilla Dynasty: Politics and Leadership in North Korea*, Boulder, CO: Westview Press, 1999, p. 31, Table 2.1.

83. Buzo asserts "[T]he chief motive for convening the congress was to publicly confer high Party office on Kim Jong Il." *Ibid.*, p. 111.

84. Suh, *Kim Il-Sung*, Chapter 15.

85. On the former, see *ibid.*, Chapter 11.

86. On dissent generally, see Oh and Hassig, *North Korea*, pp. 145-147. On specific reports of leaflets, posters, and talk, see "Dissident Leaflets Are Reported Scattered in North Korea," *New York Times* (national edition), August 24, 1994; Shim Jae Hoon, "North Korea: A Crack in the Wall," *Far Eastern Economic Review*, April 29, 1999, p. 11; and an Associated Press report dated January 19, 2005.

87. Kelly Koh and Glenn Baek, "North Korean Defectors: A Window into a Reunified Korea," in Kongdan Oh and Ralph C. Hassig, *Korea Briefing, 2000-2001: First Steps Toward Reconciliation and Reunification*, Armonk, NY: M. E. Sharpe, 2002, pp. 205-225. The statistics come from Figure 1b on p. 210.

88. Martin, *Under the Loving Care of the Fatherly Leader*, p. 539.

89. Andrei Lankov, "North Korea: Amnesty for the Kims and Their Kith," *International Herald Tribune*, January 11, 2005.

90. Selig Harrison, *Endgame in Korea*, Princeton University Press, 2002, p. 25 ff.

91. Daniel A. Pinkston, "Domestic Politics and Stakeholders in the North Korean Missile Development Program," *Nonproliferation Review*, Vol. 10, Summer 2003, pp. 51-65.

92. I wish to thank Captain John Sanford for pointing out this possibility.

93. Albright, with Woodward, *Madam Secretary*, p. 465.

94. Buzo, *The Guerilla Dynasty*, p. 56.

95. See the classic study by Albert O. Hirschmann, *Exit, Voice, Loyalty: Responses to Decline in Firms, Organizations, and States*, Cambridge, MA: Harvard University Press, 1970.

96. Maass, "The Last Emperor," p. 129.

97. See Armstrong, *The North Korean Revolution*, p. 207.

98. See Armstrong, *The North Korean Revolution*, chapter 7. "Regime of Surveillance" is the title of the chapter.

99. Armstrong, *The North Korean Revolution*, p. 208.

100. Oh and Hassig, *North Korea*, p. 191.

101. *Ibid.*, p. 88. Of course, the culture of gift giving is an important part of Kim Jong Il's power relations with all members of the elite. Martin, *Under the Loving Care of the Fatherly Leader*, pp. 275-276.

102. Martin, *Under the Loving Care of the Fatherly Leader*, p. 547.

103. Oh and Hassig, *North Korea*, pp. 119-120.

104. Scalapino and Lee, *Communism in Korea*, 1:375.

105. See Armstrong, *The North Korean Revolution*, chapter 3.

106. On the 1950s and 1960s, see Suh, *Kim Il-sung*, chapter 9.

107. James Brooke, "City Workers Sent to N. Korean Farms," *International Herald Tribune*, June 2, 2005. Of course, this is nothing unusual in North Korea or for other communist regimes. Pyongyang has done this in previous years, and it remains common practice in Cuba and was standard operating procedure in the former Soviet Union.

108. Hunter, *Kim Il-Sung's North Korea*, p. 46.

109. *Ibid.*, chapters 5, 6, and 10. On the length of military service reaching 10 years (or more), see Oh and Hassig, *North Korea*, p. 123.

110. Armstrong, *The North Korean Revolution*, pp. 72-73. See also Hunter, *Kim Il-sung's North Korea*, chapter 1.

111. This is at the core of what Scott Snyder contends are the "key themes" of the "psychological character" of Kim Il Sung and hence of North Korea's leaders. See his *Negotiating on the Edge: North Korean Negotiating Behavior*, Washington, DC: United States Institute of Peace, 1999, p. 22.

112. Armstrong, *The North Korean Revolution*, p. 27.

113. Buzo, *The Guerilla Dynasty*.

114. Armstrong, *The North Korean Revolution*, p. 36. Even Selig Harrison agrees on this point. See *Korean Endgame*, chapter 2.

115. The word "neo-traditionalist" is used by Armstrong in relation to North Korea's strict social stratification. See his *The North Korean Revolution*, p. 73.

116. As Armstrong notes, the DPRK reinforces potent aspects of "traditional Korea politics and culture" especially Confucianism. *Ibid.*, p. 6.

117. Tong Kim, "You Say Okjeryok, I Say Deterrent: No Wonder We Don't Agree," *Washington Post*, September 25, 2005. Specifically, Kim suggests that Kim Jong Il might not just be spouting propaganda when he says denuclearizing the peninsula was his father's "fervent wish."

118. A perusal of Kim Il Sung's official multivolume memoirs makes this clear. At least six volumes of his memoirs have been ghost written and published in English the 1990s. See Kim Il Sung, *With the Century*, 6 volumes, Pyongyang: Foreign Languages Publishing House, 1992-95.

119. Breen dubs it "the mother of all personality cults." See his *Kim Jong Il: North Korea's Dear Leader*, p. 5. See also Hunter, *Kim Il-sung's North Korea*, chapter 2.

120. Hunter, *Kim Il-Sung's North Korea*, p. 25.

121. See, for example, Oh and Hassig, *North Korea*, p. 100.

122. Adrian Buzo labels the regime a "Kimist System," while Stephen Bradner dubs it the "Kim Family Regime." For the former, see Buzo, *The Guerilla Dynasty*; for the latter, see Stephen Bradner, "North Korea's Strategy," in Henry D. Sokolski, ed., *Planning for a Peaceful Korea*, Carlisle Barracks, PA: U.S. Army War College, Strategic Studies Institute, 2001, pp. 23-82.

123. Albright, with Woodward, *Madam Secretary*, p. 464.

124. I am indebted to Colonel Dwight Raymond for this possible explanation.

125. Cumings, "The Corporate State in North Korea," pp. 213, 214. Coincidentally, a 2005 British documentary on North Korea is titled "A State of Mind." For a review, see Dana Stevens, "North Korea as Glimpsed Through a Spectacle," *New York Times* (Washington edition), August 10, 2005.

126. Andrew Scobell, *North Korea's Strategic Intentions*, Carlisle Barracks, PA: U.S. Army War College, Strategic Studies Institute, July 2005, p 14.

127. Martin, *Under the Loving Care of the Fatherly Leader*, pp. 522-523.

128. According to the U.S. Department of State, the literacy rate in North Korea is 99 percent. See "Background Note: North Korea" available at *www.state.gov/r/pa/ei/bgn/2782.htm*, accessed November 2, 2005. On years of compulsory schooling, see Hunter, *Kim Il-Sung's North Korea*, p. 208.

129. Martin, *Under the Loving Care of the Fatherly Leader*, p. 380; and Hunter, *Kim Il-Sung's North Korea*, p. 218.

130. Lankov, "North Korean Refugees in Northeast China," pp. 872-873.

131. As many as 15,000 North Koreans work in camps in Siberia. The figure is cited by Martin, *Under the Loving Care of the Fatherly Leader*, p. 425. For a discussion of these camps in the Russian Far East, see *ibid.*, chapter 22.

132. L. Gordon Flake and Scott Snyder, *Paved with Good Intentions: The NGO Experience in North Korea*, Westport, CT: Praeger, 2003.

133. Cited in James Brooke, "How Electronics are Penetrating North Korea's Isolation: Secret Cellphones, Smuggled Tapes," *New York Times* (Washington edition), March 15, 2005.

134. *Ibid.*

135. Rebecca MacKinnon, "North Korea: Chinese Cell Phones Spawn An Information Boom," *International Herald Tribune*, January 25, 2005.

136. On the incident and the speculation surrounding it, see "Cell Phones Spark 'Communication Revolution' in North Korea," *Chosun Ilbo*, December 3, 2004; James Brooke, "North Korea Raises Idea of a Kim III," *International Herald Tribune*, February 1, 2005; Sergey Soukhoukov, "Train Blast was 'a Plot to Kill North Korea's Leader'," report filed June 13, 2004, available at *www.telegraph.co.uk* and accessed on August 3, 2004.

137. "Why North Korea is Prohibiting Mobile Phones," *Dong A Ilbo,* May 31, 2005; and "Crackdowns, Public Executions on Sino-Korean Border," *Chosun Ilbo*, March 10, 2005.

138. Barbara Demick, "North Koreans Attend Ideology 101: Lectures Smuggled Out Show the Regime's Efforts to Combat Outside Influences Seeping in and Illustrate the Extent of Anti-Americanism," *Los Angeles Times*, December 24, 2005.

139. Brooke, "How Electronics are Penetrating North Korea's Isolation."

140. See, for example, Kang Chol-Hwan and Pierre Rigoulot, *The Aquariums of Pyongyang: Ten Years in the North Korean Gulag*, translated by Yair Reiner, New York: Basic Books, 2001, pp. 184-187. There are also many examples given by the defectors interviewed by Bradley Martin in *Under the Loving Care of the Fatherly Leader*.

141. On the spiral of silence, see Elizabeth Noelle-Neumann, "Spiral of Silence: A Theory of Public Opinion," *Journal of Communication*, Vol. 24, 1974, pp. 43-51. For an application of the concept to explain the course of events in China in 1989, see Xinshu Zhao and Peilu Shen, "Some Reasons Why the Party Propaganda Failed This Time," in Roger V. Des Forges, *et al.*, eds., *Chinese Democracy and the Crisis of 1989: Chinese and American Reflections*, Albany, NY: State University of New York Press, 1993, pp. 314-316.

142. Vladimir Tismaneanu, *Stalinism for All Seasons: A Political History of Romanian Communism*, Berkeley and Los Angeles, CA: University of California Press, 2003, pp. 230-231. Of course, the actual uprising of 1989 originated in the city of Timisoara a week earlier.

143. According to Bradley Martin, "George Orwell's 1984 is no more literary fantasy. If you were North Korean, Big Brother would watch you." Martin, *Under the Loving Care of the Fatherly Leader*, p. 265.

144. Three generations of the family would be incarcerated for the sins of one member of one generation. See *ibid.*, Chapter 16.

145. Kang and Rigoulot, *The Aquariums of Pyongyang*, p. 188.

146. The pervasiveness of corruption is evident from *ibid.*

147. For example, now families of defectors reportedly are being sent to the mountains rather than to prison camps. Still, it is debatable whether foraging in the mountains is much better than internment in a camp. Martin, *Under the Loving Care of the Fatherly Leader*, p. 572.

148. On the shortage economy concept, see, for example, Janos Kornai, *The Socialist System: The Political Economy of Communism*, Princeton, NJ: Princeton University Press, 1992, pp. 233-234.

149. Armstrong, *The North Korean Revolution*, p. 157.

150. Andrew S. Natsios, *The Great North Korean Famine: Famine, Politics, and Foreign Policy*, Washington, DC: United States Institute of Peace, 2001.

151. Scobell, *Making Sense of North Korea*, pp. 10-11.

152. This is a U.S. intelligence estimate. See the Central Intelligence Agency's *World Factbook* available on line at *www.cia.gov/cia/publications/factbook/print/kn.html*, accessed November 1, 2005.

153. Merideth Woo-Cummings, *The Political Ecology of Famine: The North Korean Catastrophe and Its Lessons*, Tokyo: Asian Development Bank, 2001.

154. Scott Snyder, "The NGO Experience in North Korea," p. 9; L. Gordon Flake, "The Experience of U.S. NGOs in North Korea," pp. 36-37; Michael Sclons, "The European NGO Experience in North Korea," pp. 53, 74; Scott Snyder, "Lessons of the NGO Experience in North Korea," p. 119, all in Flake and Snyder, eds., *Paved with Good Intentions*.

155. Andrei Lankov, "North Korea Hungry for Control," *Asia Times*, September 10, 2005.

156. James Brooke, "North Korea Says Bumper Crop Justifies Limits on Aid," *New York Times* (Washington edition), October 6, 2005.

157. *Ibid.*; and Bruce Wallace, "N. Korea Will Allow Some Aid Groups to Stay, Richardson Says," *Los Angeles Times*, October 21, 2005.

158. Donald Kirk, "North Korea Closing Another Door This Time on Food," *Christian Science Monitor*, October 18, 2005; Brooke, "North Korea Says Bumper Crop Justifies Limits on Aid."

159. Cited in Brooke, "North Korea Says Bumper Crop Justifies Limits on Aid."

160. On recent efforts to tinker with the economy, see Martin, *Under the Loving Care of the Fatherly Leader*, Chapter 35.

161. See, for example, Hunter, *Kim Il-sung's North Korea*, chapter 13 which is titled "Working to Death: An exhausted population." This chapter focuses on the tribulations of North Korean women, but the thrust of the chapter can be applied to both sexes.

162. Ken Jowitt, "Soviet Neotraditionalism: The Political Corruption of a Leninist Regime," *Soviet Studies*, Vol. XXXV, No. 3, July 1983, pp. 275-297.

163. Scobell, "Making Sense of North Korea," p. 247.

164. Recent indications are that Kim Jong Il's 20-something son, Kim Jong Chol, is being groomed to succeed his father. The younger Kim is rumored to have been introduced to Chinese President Hu Jintao during the latter's visit to Pyongyang in October 2005.